Education – An 'Impossible Profession'?

In classrooms and lectures we learn not only about academic topics but also about ourselves, our peers and how people and ideas interact. *Education – An 'Impossible Profession'?* extends the ways in which we might think about these processes by offering a refreshing reconsideration of key educational experiences including:

- being judged and assessed, both formally and informally,
- adapting to different groups for different purposes,
- struggling to think under pressure, and
- learning to recognise and adapt to the expectations of others.

The book brings psychoanalysis to new audiences, graphically illustrating its importance to understandings of teaching, learning and classrooms. Drawing on the author's original research, it considers the classroom context, including policy demands and professional pressures, and the complexity of peer and pedagogic relationships and interactions, asking how these might be being experienced and what implications such experiences might have for learners and teachers.

The discussions will be of interest not only to teachers, leading-learners and teacher-educators, but also to individuals interested in education policy, professional practice and theories of education.

Tamara Bibby is lecturer in Learning and Teaching at the Institute of Education, University of London, UK.

Foundations and Futures of Education

Series Editors:
Peter Aggleton *School of Education and Social Work, University of Sussex, UK*
Sally Power *Cardiff University, UK*
Michael Reiss *Institute of Education, University of London, UK*

Foundations and Futures of Education focuses on key emerging issues in education, as well as continuing debates within the field. The series is interdisciplinary, and includes historical, philosophical, sociological, psychological and comparative perspectives on three major themes: the purposes and nature of education; increasing interdisciplinarity within the subject; and the theory–practice divide.

Language, Learning, Context
Wolff-Michael Roth

Learning, Context and the Role of Technology
Rosemary Luckin

Education and the Family
Passing success across the generations
Leon Feinstein, Kathryn Duckworth and Ricardo Sabates

Education, Philosophy and the Ethical Environment
Graham Haydon

Educational Activity and the Psychology of Learning
Judith Ireson

Schooling, Society and Curriculum
Alex Moore

Gender, Schooling and Global Social Justice
Elaine Unterhalter

Education – An 'Impossible Profession'?

Psychoanalytic explorations of learning and classrooms

Tamara Bibby

Routledge
Taylor & Francis Group

LONDON AND NEW YORK

First published 2011
by Routledge
2 Park Square, Milton Park, Abingdon, Oxon OX14 4RN

Simultaneously published in the USA and Canada
by Routledge
270 Madison Avenue, New York, NY 10016

Routledge is an imprint of the Taylor & Francis Group, an informa business

© 2011 Tamara Bibby

Typeset in Garamond by Swales & Willis Ltd, Exeter, Devon
Printed and bound in Great Britain by CPI Antony Rowe, Chippenham, Wiltshire

British Library Cataloguing in Publication Data
A catalogue record for this book is available from the British Library

Library of Congress Cataloging-in-Publication Data
A catalog record has been requested for this book

ISBN13: 978–0–415–55265–3 (hbk)
ISBN13: 978–0–415–55266–0 (pbk)
ISBN13: 978–0–203–84445–8 (ebk)

Contents

Acknowledgements

I would like to thank the Economic and Social Research Council (ESRC) for funding the research project 'Children's learner identities in mathematics at Key Stage 2' (Award number: RES-000-22-1272). Although this book is not a report of that research, it draws on the data that the team collected and the thinking I undertook during and after the project. I would like to thank colleagues at King's College London and the Institute of Education, London who helped me write the original proposal and the team (Sheryl Clark, Alice Haddon and Alex Moore) who worked with me on the project. Many thanks also go to the staff and pupils of 'Grafton School' who granted us access to their classrooms and learning processes.

Many people have been involved with aspects of the work presented here. I would also like to thank all those who have been generous with their time and energy and have read and commented on earlier drafts of chapters. Particular thanks are due to Peter Aggleton, Margaret Bibby, Sheryl Clark, Alan Cribb, Julian Grenier, Alice Haddon, Claudia Lapping, Helen Lucey, Meg Maguire, Alex Moore, Anne Murray, Caroline Pelletier, Ros Sills and Gordon Stobart.

I would also like to thank Sense Publishers for permission to reuse parts of a chapter published by them. My description of Jessica Benjamin's work (used in chapter 8) was previously published in *The Psychology of Mathematics Education: A Psychoanalytic Displacement* edited by Tony Brown.

Gratitude is also due to friends whose delightful distraction contributed to any balance I managed to maintain over the course of the research, thinking and writing: Chris, Czech, Janice, Gus, Sarah, Onion, Tina, Lillian, Luci, Claire, Chloe, Kevin, Harry, Steve, Alison *et al.* Thank you all very much.

1 An introduction

Where this book comes from

For many years, first as a teacher and later as a researcher and teacher educator, the psychology I engaged with was dominated by the work of Skinner, Piaget and Vygotsky, and later that of Jerome Bruner. The work of these cognitive psychologists was undoubtedly useful in that it provided me with models and metaphors to think about aspects of learning and development, processes central to education (Moore, 2000). For example, school and classroom behaviour management: rules and sanctions, 'golden time', reward charts, stickers and assemblies that praise good work are all educational applications (and misapplications) of Skinnerian operant conditioning. Yet somehow, despite the attractive promise of sticker charts and table points, in the hustle and bustle of the classroom and in schools that must perform to succeed, it seems easier to pounce on and punish the negative than it is to recognise and reward the positive (Parsons, 2005). Skinner would be spinning in his grave.

Piaget thought of himself as a genetic epistemologist, interested in the development of knowledge. His ages and stages of development were never intended for educational purposes yet they influence the structure and content of schooling including the National Curriculum. This despite the fact that his work has been consistently criticised for experimental and interpretive inaccuracies (Donaldson, 1978; Hughes, 1986; Tizard and Hughes, 1984), and for the unintended and unfortunate side effects of their application in creating and perpetuating notions of 'normal' and 'natural' children and childhood development (Burman, 1994, 1997; Walkerdine, 1984). Vygotsky's and Bruner's introduction to psychology of sociocultural stories is to be welcomed. These theories broadened the basis of our decisions about children and their learning although they still rely on tales of rational, linear development (Bibby, 2008), of normal and smoothly developing children and rational, logical teachers knowing and acting in the child's best interests.

For me, the tension between the utter difficulty of being in the classroom and the calm, rational responses of those writing about learning and teaching grew and became increasingly difficult to live with. But I did not want to be told how to fix my perceived problems; I was not necessarily sure I agreed about where the 'problems' lay. Idealised and generalised classrooms seemed to offer me nothing but endless personal and professional failure – why could I not make it all work like I was (apparently) supposed to? Still, the muddle and chaos, the delight of the triumphs and the despair of the difficulties all seemed important – in them lay the vital heart of classroom life. Would I really want to teach, work or live in classrooms where children never fell out, never got furious with each other and me, didn't push and test the boundaries, didn't refuse to learn or find learning impossible? What would that mean? Would I want never to be asked a question I couldn't answer? A fix seemed to threaten to remove the passion and creativity, the inquisitive questioning and the excitement from the children and also from me, from the relationships that drive learning in classrooms. And so I turned to a different body of literature and a different form of psychological understanding – to psychoanalytic theories and the struggle to hold together both the love and the hate, the desire and the fear.

But why psychoanalysis? I gradually became frustrated with the increasingly narrow understanding of education that I was expected to work with. Schools, colleges and universities are all guilty of this reduction – if only because we demand it of them. An open, broad understanding of education, of learning from paintings, novels and films, of learning from our friendships and enmities and from the labours of life seems to be a far cry from what happens in formal places of learning, or at least what is called learning in those places. We elevate the serious business of 'work' above an infantilised notion of 'play' and, despite protestations about lifelong learning, are quick to limit learning to something that happens in school – what a relief we do not have to do that again, all that painful growing up and passing all those useless exams!

Deborah Britzman has characterised formal education as an encounter with 'an avalanche of certainty' (2009: 2), an encounter with certain knowledge, with tests and measures of success and failure. It is worth considering her evocative description of the strange disappointments and frustrations of being a teacher:

> Many accept the fact that we do not know what is going on or even how we feel about it, that students puzzle us or make us mad, and that however much we plan in advance, however clear our lesson plans feel to us, whatever beauty our syllabus design mirrors, however narcissistic we may feel in conveying knowledge or however much we attempt to convey our understanding to others or strain to receive the other's inchoate views, the pedagogical encounter and what becomes of it are radically unstable, subject to the unconscious and the dream work.
>
> (Britzman, 2009: xi)

This honest highlighting of the fact that so much of what happens in the formal classroom is beyond our control is tantamount to heresy in the current context of learning and teaching in England. The need to control, ensure, demonstrate that our students have 'met their learning objectives' and (in a strange piece of mathematical unthink) are all achieving at or above the expected average is the rhetorical force shaping our endeavours. The complete denial of the reality of classroom life and of learning makes it impossible to think about broader, more enduring notions of education and learning. Or, as Britzman points out, perhaps it is the pull of our own experiences of formal learning that drags our minds back to memories of our schooling, that shrinks and limits what education can be. Perhaps the wild possibilities of what education might be are just too threatening?

In this respect, it is notable that the qualification to become a head teacher in England (the National Professional Qualification for Headship (NPQH)) is now a competency-based qualification and that this replaces past requirements for classroom experience and later a master's degree in education: the control has ratcheted up; the possibilities for what counts as valuable learning for a teacher to become a leader or manager of teachers have reduced as the requirements have been listed and quantified. We circle the drain: we want education and learning to be 'more' but then *how do we know it will be useful or appropriate?* What is useful and appropriate? Better list it, then we can check if the important stuff has been learned. And the rest? Well, it would be nice but we do not have time, and it does not appear on the list of what is important and useful. And even so the curriculum is overcrowded, better trim it down. Perhaps this bit is a little less vital than that bit, perhaps we can do without it . . .

To begin to make sense of this and other education-based contractions, of these reductions and minimisings, we will need to think differently. To not get sucked into the naming and measuring, the acting and blaming, the swapping of this constraint for that restriction, to step aside and think about *why*, at some level, we feel compelled to collude and perpetuate these normalised contractions, requires a different set of tools and a different language. That is why psychoanalysis seems attractive. It can provide different sets of metaphors and give attention to the difficult bits: the fears and anxieties, the fantasies and desires, the loves and hates, the less than rational and the strange logics of our passions and our unconsciouses. It enables, indeed it requires, us to say the unsayable, to experience what it feels like to utter the forbidden words, and to know that the unbearable feelings are in us as they are in others. Because, I suggest, that is where we need to go to try to make some sense of why education is, as Freud suggested, an impossible profession.

Anna O[1] famously characterised her experience of psychoanalysis as a 'talking cure' but we need to be careful how we understand her statement since psychoanalysis does not hold out 'cures' in the medical sense of that word. When life is difficult and painful the thought that someone can smooth over the bumps or forever erase the pain is very attractive. And indeed pain can be modified, yet some trace, some memory of it will remain and continue to affect our lives. There is no route map for an easy walk through life's vicissitudes, but I will suggest that there may be some ideas that can help us to think about the difficulties and why they might feel so hard, or downright impossible, to deal with. And that in turn can help us to develop some ideas for other ways of thinking and acting – if we can bear it. And, maybe, sometimes we can't, and that too will need to be borne. So this book aims to explore such paradoxical difficulties and will draw on ideas from a variety of psychoanalytic theorists to do so.

What it is and what it is not

In the course of the chapters in this book I explore aspects of education and class-room life with a range of psychoanalytic lenses. While the book does not assume any prior knowledge of psychoanalysis or psychoanalytic theory it is not a 'primer' and does not explain the basics of all theories nor their historical genesis and inter-relations. If that is your interest, or if it becomes your interest, then Elliott (2002), Elliott and Frosh (1995) and Frosh (1999) are useful places to start. Nor is it a guide to 'therapeutic education' or the claims of Richard Layard (2006, 2007) and others that we can and should teach children to be happy. These claims and sug-gestions rely on the use of 'cognitive, behavioural therapy' (CBT) and have gener-ated long-running debates in the media (O'Hara, 2005; Shepherd, 2009) and drawn fierce criticism from academics who complain that attempts to 'teach hap-piness' distort the purposes of education and create a culture of vulnerability (Ecclestone and Hayes, 2009; Furedi, 2004).

But we need to be careful here. CBT and psychotherapy or psychoanalysis are widely different projects. That they can all sit under the broad umbrella of 'ther-apy' is misleading and unhelpful. CBT can enable people to learn to rationalise and so try to find ways beyond aspects of their lives that are creating difficulties for them. Typically CBT has been used to support people with issues such as stopping smoking, coming to terms with drug or alcohol abuse, mild depression, or bereavement. It sets identifiable goals in an explicit and conscious way and tends to be conducted in a time-limited context (for example six sessions provided by the National Health Service (NHS)). Its short time-span, identifiable targets and measurable outcomes make it seem ideal in the current culture of targets and cost-effectiveness. Yet the government's recent enthusiastic embrace of CBT[2] has the feel of a child's desire for someone with a wand to magic the difficulties away, a pied-piper to remove all the nasty rats. When we are happy, the policy story goes, we can be economically useful rather than a drain on the public purse. This is a problematic fantasy for at least two reasons. First, it assumes that people who are not 'happy' are economically or socially unproductive; a wrong and deeply trou-bling assumption. Second, CBT does not always work and it does not work for everyone – an underlying problem can re-emerge elsewhere and CBT has no way of managing this apart from treating the re-emergence as a new problem.

Psychoanalysis, in contrast to CBT, works with the unconscious and may con-tinue for years. It is a long and unpredictable journey that requires patience, com-mitment and courage. As such it is not for everyone and certainly the NHS would struggle to fund it. It is also a practice that requires long training for its practitioners and it cannot be undertaken quickly. There are books (Bollas, 1999) and TV series such as *In Treatment* (Garcia, 2008) that describe the journey of psychoanalytic psychotherapies if that is of interest to you. However, this book is not about a personal analytic journey in that sense. Rather, following a tradition of work in cultural studies, art, anthropology and education, it uses the tools developed for clinical work to explore social processes. We need to heed the words of Sigmund and Anna Freud, Susan Isaacs and others: psychoanalysis and education are different projects, they work differently. Psychoanalysis cannot provide a prophylactic for education although it can provide tools and metaphors for thinking about education. That is a fine distinction, but it is an important one.

Psychoanalytic theory can sometimes be dense and difficult to understand. Typically it is written in terms of clinical practice, often the intense one-to-one relationship of the analyst and the client or patient. For some readers such language may not sit easily in a book about learning in the classroom, teachers and students, adults and children. So while this book is not a straight 'report of research', I will draw on classroom-based research I have been involved in to contextualise, reframe and develop ideas from psychoanalytic theory.

The aspects of learning and classroom life chosen for consideration reflect my own interests and concerns. They are not the only difficulties that could have been chosen, and similarly, the theories or aspects of theories that I draw on are not the only ones. Those that I have selected have been shaped by my history as a primary school teacher and my research which has largely taken place in primary school classrooms and has often focussed on mathematics lessons. Despite this apparently narrow focus, I suspect the issues will be familiar to people who work in other kinds of classrooms – they continue to resonate for me in seminars at all levels in higher education, from foundation degree to doctoral work. The work of education is not time-limited or age-specific, whatever our fantasies about schooling might suggest and however they may return us to forgetfulness.

Throughout this book I will resist any suggestion that there is a cure or a simple fix to the difficulties of learning in formal contexts. I will view magic wands and fairy-dust with suspicion and wonder why they still seem attractive when we know they don't exist and don't work. I do not restrict myself to one school of psychoanalytic thought, but draw widely and without apology. An aim of this book is to raise more questions – what would happen if I applied those ideas to this other issue? Why are those ideas useful here, what would that other theorist have said? – and invite others to engage with answering them, but that will not be the purpose of this book.

Key ideas

As I indicated earlier, psychoanalysis is a complex field with a specialist vocabulary. Words can mean different things in everyday and psychoanalytic usage and these differences can create problems for some readers. Many of these problems revolve around the way psychoanalysis moves between literal and metaphorical language. Reading about envy, denial, the phallus, a good breast, a child's death-wish and so on can be uncomfortable if we assume they are being used with their everyday literal connotations; I will discuss these difficulties as they arise. Throughout the book, I will work to enable you to gain some understanding of the specialist meaning of the words and concepts I draw on. Like all definitions, though, there is always room for more nuanced and detailed understandings.

A first important idea is that psychoanalytic ideas are not monolithic. Given the length of his career it is perhaps to be expected that there are important differences within Freud's own writings which came about as his ideas developed and changed. Unsurprisingly there are also significant differences between Freud and those who worked with his ideas in different ways and in different places. Those who interpret any theorist will find points of agreement and bones of contention with those they interpret and amongst their peers and colleagues. In fact, like any area of interest there are different schools of thought with many apparent similarities and major differences. As I said earlier, I will not be exploring these debates and arguments here although they are interesting and informative in themselves and have been extensively discussed elsewhere (see for example Britzman's (2003) discussion of the debates between Anna Freud and Melanie Klein).

Despite this ferment and fracturing of the historical and professional stories of psychoanalysis, it still rests on some key ideas. The ways these are presented and the language used vary and the emphasis may change amongst the schools and theorists but in general terms we need to accept some broad principles as we move into the chapters of this book:

- that we possess a dynamic unconscious that we can never access directly or know completely;
- that we are constituted with defences, we are 'defended subjects'; and
- that not only does our unconscious affect us and those around us, society and culture also shape our unconscious, that is, we are psychosocial beings.

Each of these is discussed in more detail hereafter.

The dynamic unconscious

The radical suggestion at the heart of all psychoanalysis is that the mind is split into that part which is conscious of the self, the 'I' that knows I am sitting typing these words and is conscious of the nagging discomfort in my back and the cars on the road outside, and the unconscious part that I cannot access. That means that there is a part of me that is not known to me: other people may get glimpses of this other part in mismatches between things that I say and do or moods I appear to project and the way I seem to them, but they too cannot know my (or their) unconscious. I may get some sense of my unconscious in my slips and forgettings and, above all, in my dreams although without undertaking psycho-analysis I am unlikely to make much sense of these (it is, after all, material I have repressed). Freud makes a careful distinction between what he terms the *precon-scious*, that which is 'latent and capable of becoming conscious' (Freud, 1923), those words or ideas that hover on the tip-of-the-tongue that can't be recalled for the moment, and the properly unconscious, that which is repressed and funda-mentally unknowable.

This notion of an unknown and fundamentally unknowable unconscious can be unsettling as it wrests the illusion of our self-control and self-knowledge from us. As Stephen Frosh explains:

> What we are taught to see as 'natural' in the human condition, the capacity to use *reason*, is only a small part of the story: behind every action is a wish, behind every thought is an unreasonable desire. Psychoanalysis thus chal-lenges the Western view that the distinguishing mark of humanity is reason and rationality, arguing instead that the human 'essence' lies in unacceptable and hence repressed impulses towards sexuality and aggression.
>
> (Frosh, 2002: 17, emphasis in the original)

Common sense (non-psychoanalytic) understandings of the unconscious vary but often portray it as static and little-changing, a repository for things we don't want to know about. Sometimes it is anthropomorphised and turned into a wilful homunculus driving our actions. But for Freud the unconscious was a place of great energy and movement – it is dynamic. The dynamism takes two forms. First there is repression; the unconscious presses the unknowable away from our awareness and keeps it there although the thought fights back. The more danger-ous the knowledge or thought, the more forcefully it is held down. Second it is dynamic in the generative, creative sense that it causes or generates dreams and phantasies.[3] These dreams and our fantasies, our conscious or preconscious dreams and wishes developed dynamically from the unconscious, assist in the process of repression by holding out something enticing to keep our focus away from the terrifying. For Freud the unconscious is more active, dynamic and ener-getic than the conscious mind; precisely because it does not have to pay attention to reality, it can be as wild and unfettered as it will.

What we can know of the unconscious comes through observing its effects in analysis; meaning is developed in the analytic relationship through a process of free-association. The patterns, echoes and affects of this process are where the effects of the unconscious, of the psychic life of the individual, come to be par-tially known. They can never be completely known, not least because the uncon-scious is dynamic, it doesn't sit still and wait to be known, and knowing this bit changes it to some degree:

> The forbidden wishes and all the phantasies connected with them constitute the core of what is called 'psychic reality'. This concept replaced Freud's first

idea that some actual occurrence such as seduction in childhood caused the later production of neurotic symptoms. Unconscious processes completely replace external reality (with which they have no truck) by psychical reality. Psychical reality is not commensurate with an inner world in general or with all psychological productions; it is a hard core, a nugget, felt to be as real as the grass and the trees, as real as (and not unconnected with) the fact that one is born to two parents and is either a boy or a girl.

(Mitchell, 1998: 22)

This introduction of a new idea, *psychic reality*, is important and links with the suggestion later that we are *psychosocial*:

psychic reality is what the subject *lives in*; this replaces an abstracted opposition of the 'outer' as against the 'inner' with a conceptualisation of the 'psychic' as that which stands in for both … [T]he subject is always immersed in a flux that is neither inside nor outside, but something else – a folding of space that is perhaps closer to the Moebius ideal.

(Frosh and Baraitser, 2008: 354, emphasis in the original)

The metaphorical image or structure of the unconscious, what is believed to be repressed and precisely how repression acts vary according to theorist. However, repressed aspects of the unconscious will often relate to sexuality and aggression. Envy, hatred, love and guilt are all emotions arising out of the ways in which repressed aspects of our selves influence what we can and cannot know, do and say. Keeping ourselves bearable and acceptable in our own eyes requires that we defend ourselves against these unbearable, repressed aspects and the anxiety they constantly provoke.

The defended subject

To suggest that someone is being defensive is, in everyday parlance, to accuse them of an unnecessary or unpleasant action. An accusation of defensiveness derides someone's rejection of our good sense or astute observation. It is a dismissal of a refusal to agree and a simultaneous claim to authority. But in psychoanalysis defence implies no criticism, it is a statement of constitutive fact not a pejorative judgement.

Our defences develop as a way to manage the anxieties provoked by the difficult experiences of living and processing life, the difficulty of managing our conscious and unconscious lives. Walkerdine, Lucey and Melody explain:

At the conscious level anxieties may be named and talked about. But at the level of the unconscious, rather than being 'out of sight, out of mind', anxieties continue to wield their considerable power beyond the rationalising influence of language.

(2001: 89–90)

Just because we can't name and speak our unconscious anxieties does not mean that we do not live with them: the many-tentacled existential terrors of vulnerability and dependence and so forth. So unconscious anxieties and fears lead to distortions in the ways in which we story our lives for ourselves and for others; they colour our dreams, shape our desires, deflect our actions, and impact our friendships and our daily decisions. They develop from real or imagined experiences and continue to accrete through life.

It is Kleinian psychoanalysis that most carefully and productively charts this defended subject. The processes central to defending the self from all that is unbearable are denial, splitting and projection. I deal with each very briefly here; they will continue to be explored later. Walkerdine, Lucey and Melody explain that *denial* is, like other unconscious process, concerned with the 'management and regulation of anxiety'. They define it as involving 'a refusal to recognise or appreciate the inner significance of an experience' (Walkerdine, Lucey and Melody, 2001: 91). It is one of a series of ways of dealing with an anxiety, often accompanied by splitting and projection. *Splitting* is a way of protecting things that are experienced as good (nourishing, affirming, loving, capable, secure, etc.) from being contaminated with things we experience as bad (dangerous, anxiety-provoking, envious, angry, hating, etc.). To keep that which is 'good' safe we can either *project* the good onto the Other and have them act as a safe place while we hold on to the part felt to be dangerous (a situation that, psychoanalytically, exemplifies envy), or we can keep the good to ourselves and *project* the bad onto the Other (Mitchell, 1998). In this way we can safely experience our own negative emotions. (Of course, it is possible the other person does not feel whatever we are projecting onto them and they may be startled at our inappropriate reaction to them.)

The processes are somewhat more complex that that. Life never only operates in one direction, and unconscious communication, like the more familiar conscious communication, is received as well as generated. So processes of introjection, of taking in, accompany processes of projection, and we may gladly receive certain types of projection although this will vary from person to person. Other unconscious processes, particularly of identification and projective identification, are also implicated in the life of the defended subject. These ideas will be explored and developed more fully in later chapters.

We are psychosocial beings

In everyday life as well as in much social science, there is a tendency to drift into thinking about things as either internal and individual or external, social events. Such a distinction might enable us to decide, for example, to study *either* psychology *or* sociology. Yet this dichotomising is a form of splitting and misses the ways in which the internal and the external, the private and public, the individual and social are deeply mutually implicated:

Unconscious processes, while remaining hidden, nevertheless profoundly influence and are intertwined with more conscious processes; not only individual and social ones, but also the very structures of collective human life – material and ideological institutions such as the state, education, the family and work; the organisation of biological processes such as motherhood; the lived experiences of class, race and femininity.

(Walkerdine, Lucey and Melody, 2001: 84)

The suggestion is that, not only does our unconscious affect us and those around us; so too do society and culture shape our unconscious, that is, we are psychosocial beings. In his essay 'Civilization and its discontents', Freud (1930) considers the ways this happens suggesting that, paradoxically, while civilisation is constructed to ease the difficulties of living life, it simultaneously creates other difficulties in living life. He suggests that the price of living in civilisation and having the economies of effort that group-living can bring is that we renounce many (potential) sources of pleasure. 'Civilized man', he says, 'has exchanged a portion of his possibilities of happiness for a portion of security' (Freud, 1930: 115) and in this exchange the repression of sexuality and aggression, the development of guilt and anxiety are part of the cost.

In an effort to explicate what 'psychosocial' might mean, then, Frosh and Baraitser highlight the use of the term *psychic reality* as a way of avoiding the trap of dichotomous thinking, and propose the image of the Moebius strip in which 'underside and topside, inside and outside flow together as one, and the choice of how to see them is purely tactical, just like the decision as to whether to look at the subject from the "social" or "psychological" perspective' (2008: 349). While the analyses and discussions in this book are tactically skewed to the psychoanalytically psychological, all discussions take place in an environment full of social and cultural meanings. There is always another side to be told, another opinion to be sought, another interpretation to be made.

An important early example of a psychosocial investigation is found in the work of Isabel Menzies Lyth (1960). In the late 1950s, initially tasked with exploring high rates of staff turnover and low rates of student completion in a teaching hospital, she investigated the ways in which experienced nurses, individually and as groups, acted together with the systems of the hospital to contain the unconscious anxieties of the nurses. Trainees and veteran nurses experienced anxieties relating to the fear of dependency, the unbearable intimacies of nursing care, the envy of having someone to look after your needs, the difficulty of not being able to 'fix' all the patients and so on. She found that what she called 'social defences' such as moving the trainees around regularly so they would not get too attached to individual patients, and wearing uniforms to homogenise the care given actually created more anxiety. What is particularly interesting is her detailing of the ways in which individual and group phantasies about caring, nursing, and efficiency, operated together to produce notions of professionalism and templates for action that were ultimately self-defeating. What she avoids is any story of 'good nurses' and 'bad administrators'. Rather, in intending to do the best we can fail to look at why a particular action might seem best (Best for who? Best for what purposes? What does 'worst' mean in that context? Why is that 'worst'?). Her careful detailing of the findings and the clarity of her analysis ensure that this remains a very useful study – interesting to read and a template for reflecting on the systems in other institutions.

Some difficulties with these ideas and responses to those difficulties

There have been many criticisms of psychoanalysis. Amongst these are its individualising and normalising tendencies, its focus on the male experience, especially in the Oedipus crisis, and the apparent negativity of the language. These will be dealt with as they arise but a detailed exploration and answering of each is not the purpose of this book. Debates about psychoanalysis and gender in particular are complex and have been heated, with feminist theorists having made significant contributions to our understanding of the issues (see for example, Appignanesi and Forrester, 2005; Butler, 2004; Doane and Hodges, 1993). I have elected not to point out every time an author refers to the child, or a generalised individual as masculine. Many of the psychoanalytic sources used here were written at a time when that was the convention; it no longer is but I believe the reader is able to make the necessary mental adjustments. Books such as Stephen Frosh's *The Politics of Psychoanalysis* (1999) deal systematically with the more general criticisms.

The research base of the book

The data drawn on in this book were gathered as part of a project entitled 'Children's learner-identities in mathematics at Key Stage 2'.[4] The project, which worked with one class of children, took place over five terms, from late in the summer term of 2005 (children in year 4, aged 9) to the end of the autumn term in year 6 (December 2006, children aged 10 or 11). The project team consisted of myself, Sheryl Clark, Alice Haddon and Alex Moore. Throughout the book pseudonyms are used for the school and the research participants. The children chose their own and, while these are always 'gender appropriate', they do not always clearly reflect the ethnicity of the children.

Grafton School is a highly successful multi-ethnic, inner-urban school in London. It consistently comes towards the top of the local authority league tables. The school represented the ethnic makeup of the area quite well, being about 50 per cent Bangladeshi with 30 per cent white (UK) working class and the remaining 20 per cent being of Black Caribbean, African, Chinese and Indian heritages. Around two-thirds of the pupils spoke English as an additional language. The teachers were all experienced apart from Miss South, the year 5 class teacher, who had been employed following a successful teaching placement the previous summer.

The school's intake formed two parallel classes in each year group. Each pair of classes was served by two class teachers, a support teacher and a teaching assistant (TA). In addition, the class the research was based in also had a second TA who supported one child with moderate autism. The school's practice, for both literacy and mathematics lessons, was to reconfigure the two classes in each year group to form three 'ability groups'. The three 'split' groups were taught simultaneously by the three teachers. The groups were configured differently for literacy and mathematics.[5]

The research team collected data from a number of sources including: observations of lessons with unplanned, incidental discussions with the teacher, pupils and the TAs; longer paired and group interviews with the children in the class, key members of staff connected to the class and parents of some of the children; interviews associated with drawing and photographic activities (Mauthner, 1997). Alongside these familiar adult-initiated activities we enabled the children to undertake their own research. Their research activities included questionnaires they developed and administered to their peers; and interviews with their classmates and the adults in the school. The children became involved in aspects of the production and analysis of data and this became part of the data for the larger project.

The intention of the study was to explore learning and what it means to learn from the point of view of the younger members of the class. That is to say, we followed their concerns and ways of talking about themselves and their learning rather than having an adult agenda structuring our interviews. In this way, we hoped to gain insight into their ways of knowing themselves and others through their voices.

The structure of the book

Policy metaphors and the trends associated with them have tended to sideline and make it difficult to think and talk about less rational aspects of teaching and learning. These less rational but nonetheless powerful aspects of the learning context include the desire for control and vengeance, resistance, the fear of failure (and success), peer pressure, love and hatred, loss and anxiety.

Chapter 2 draws on Menzies Lyth's study (1960) to consider the primary task of the school and the social defences of the institution. It asks what is being asked of schools and teachers and considers how these demands and expectations interact with personal biographies to generate anxieties. If, as is suggested, the primary task is taken to be the overlay of knowledge on the developing child, then what anxieties might be aroused? And how does the school, as an institution, enable its teachers to function without becoming overwhelmed? Three particular defences are considered: compliance, systematicity and fragmentation.

The following chapters take the work of one or two key theorists to explore themes relating to learning in formal contexts. Throughout, illustrative, real-life examples are provided from my own research grounding the theory in real classroom events. Chapter 3 considers the way processes of identification construct identities in learning environments. Jacques Lacan's use of a mirror metaphor is used to think about the way learners 'see' themselves in their interactions with others. The difficulties the children experienced faced with the necessity of making sense of (often impoverished) versions of themselves are explored. Chapter 4 develops the work begun in chapter 3. It widens the focus, pulling back from individual teacher/pupil exchanges to consider the context within which those exchanges took place: classrooms framed by accountability structures. Donald Winnicott's work on the holding environment is used to explore some of the difficulties children have from time to time with developing identities that enable them to learn creatively. Characteristics of a 'good-enough' holding environment are considered and compared to the environment provided by an 'accountability' classroom.

The individual nature of the learning experience is challenged in the next two chapters. Much psychoanalytic thinking, like much educational thinking, is premised on the one-to-one relationship of the analyst and analysand (teacher and child). However, S. H. Foulkes and Wilfred Bion were group psychoanalysts and have particular things to say to teachers because of their focus on one-to-many relationships such as those teachers and classes live within. Their work provides a different way of thinking about classroom dynamics and thinking in group contexts. Chapter 5 asks 'What is a group?' and considers the work groups undertake to develop and maintain their boundaries. What such work might look like and the fact that it is deemed problematic in classrooms is discussed. Chapter 6 draws on aspects of Bion's work to think in a different way about group processes. His understandings about our behaviour in groups can help us to think about and react to classroom events somewhat differently. Bion's ideas about the 'working' and 'basic assumption' groups are used to provide a different way of storying distressingly familiar events.

Following chapters on the identities of individuals and the ways we can think about how they use the classroom environment, the next two chapters shift to consider thought and thinking. Chapter 7 draws extensively on Melanie Klein's work on object relating, and Bion's understanding of the K link to theorise the thinking that takes place 'in the head'. That all such thinking is produced from flows of affect, and the suggestion that thinking and 'mind' are called into existence to cope with thoughts, challenge rational and cognitive stories about thought and thinking. Some implications for this psychoanalytically informed model of thinking are explored. Klein's theories are based on drives and internal processes which some have rejected. Starting in similar places, others developed the necessity for thinking within relationships and consider the kinds of relationships that enable, or frustrate, thinking. The works of Winnicott and Jessica Benjamin are used to provide a different story about thought and thinking. There are parallels with Klein's theories, and these are also discussed.

The final chapter considers the 'dark side' of teaching and explores some reasons why glossing over this with sentimental and idealised stories of love and self-sacrifice might be problematic. Most of the chapters in this book focus on the experience of the learner or the learner with the teacher. Chapter 9 is somewhat different as it focusses on the teacher; it returns to Winnicott to consider the desirability and possibility of moving beyond the impossible idealisations inherent in policy invocations of the effective teacher, the perfect lesson and the ideal learner. The question of what it might mean to be 'good-enough' is explored. Throughout the book, data from my research has provided rich examples of the ways in which the desires and expectations of policy, teachers and pupils are in conflict with each other and the extent to which each is 'deaf' to the other. It is the psychic and emotional costs of these 'deafnesses' that the chapter will investigate.

2   The primary task of the school?

In chapter 1, I suggested that Isabel Menzies Lyth's study (1960) of social defences in a teaching hospital might provide a useful template for reflecting on life in other institutions. In this chapter, I aim to use such an approach to develop some sense of how in education the world 'out there' enters into everyday understanding and practice, and how the world 'out there' gets into every one of us (Frosh and Baraitser, 2008). While the focus is on education as an institution, through a consideration of the anxieties provoked by education, schooling and knowledge, the discussion will highlight some ways in which social discourses interact with the psychic life of individuals. The chapters that follow will take some of these or related issues and develop them in more detail.

Menzies Lyth's analysis is in two parts. The first considers the ways in which anxiety is produced in relation to the 'primary task' of the hospital. In doing this she considers the 'objective' features of the hospital: its primary task in relation to the sick patients and their relatives, and the internal objects in the nurses' 'inner representational worlds': their own phantasies and biographies. The second part of her analysis considers the *social defences* established within the nursing service: the systems and practices put in place to alleviate anxiety. In applying this approach as a framework for reflecting on education and the roles of teachers in schools, we have two tasks. The first, paralleling her analysis, requires us to think about the 'objective features' of the school: its 'primary task' and the relations of the teachers, children and their parents[1] to that task; and the internal objects of teachers' inner representational worlds. Here, we need to consider the ways in which the anxieties experienced by teachers are inseparable from the organisational context of the school. Then, second, we need to consider the *social defences* established by aspects of the teaching and educational system to protect against and alleviate these anxieties.

The primary task of the school in relation to learners and their carers

What then is the 'primary task' of the school? This is a difficult but important question; it provides us with a way to begin to think about the investments and resistances we might harbour. From the perspective of an outsider, it seems clear that the primary task of the hospital is to care for the ill, to make them 'better', to take in the sick and discharge the well. So, what is the 'primary task' of the educational institution? While it may seem enough to say the answer is implicit in the term itself, it is to educate, this needs some development as the term is contested. What does it mean to educate or to be educated? While these are important questions, they also seem to miss the point and to deflect us into the realms of the wider social remits of education (cultural and social reproduction or self and social improvement, etc.).

It may be helpful to think of the primary task of the school as having two major dimensions: the creation, control and transmission of knowledge, and facilitating the development of the child. The school takes the young who do not know and turns them into adults who do know, so that its primary task is to overlay some notion of development with the transmission of knowledge. For those working in compulsory educational settings the work is with *all* the literally young: infants, children and young adults. But learning continues beyond schooling and into post-compulsory and informal settings. So does the primary task of the school belong only to the compulsory sector? I think not, although the language and our sense of ourselves as adults, knowers and learners may challenge an acceptance of this claim. For those working in post-compulsory settings, the label 'young' has to be understood metaphorically: a 'young' graduate emerging from the university may be mature in years but is in other ways a novice. We can imagine a learning journey, a life-course within the larger project of our lives: from 'birth' into a need to learn or an area of potential learning, 'development' through it and eventual 'graduation' from it. The way particular 'learning life-courses' overlay, and are conflated with, apparently 'natural' development seen over the course of compulsory schooling, disrupts our sense of age, notions of maturity and chronology and can make it easy for us, once we are beyond the age of compulsory schooling, to disavow any suggestion that we need to learn anything (Britzman, 2009).

The way we imagine learners traversing the plane defined by the two dimensions of the primary task – knowledge and development – will vary considerably. The desirability of sticking closely to one or the other axis, the directness of the path, tolerance for periods of apparent immobility and so forth are the stuff of beliefs and values, and are central non-rationalities at the heart of education's more rational endeavours.

How, then, might contact with educational institutions produce anxiety, and what sorts of anxieties? Menzies Lyth points out that even short conversations with people that work in, or interact with, an institution show the ways in which their conceptions of the primary task of the institution are 'a rich mixture of objective knowledge, logical deduction and fantasy' (1960: 165): things that are observably true, things that can reasonably be inferred from observations, and our imaginings (things we fancy we see, implications we desire or fear, and our defences to these). She suggests that it is fantasy that most directly influences the levels of stress and anxiety that are experienced. What fantasies might be related to the primary task of the school if we accept that this is concerned with the creation, control and transmission of knowledge, and facilitating the development of the child? What kinds of anxiety might such fantasies provoke? One fantasy might be that this task is one that is do-able! The manifold implications of that fantasy are what are explored throughout this book and are also the topics of others (see, for example, Boldt and Salvio, 2006 and Todd, 1997). In this chapter, however, we will stay close to the reflective task prompted by a reading of Menzies Lyth.

The creation, control and transmission of knowledge

The need for schools to create certainty through knowledge that can be relied upon and used wisely is substantial, and so we might expect there to be anxieties around both the creation and management of such knowledge. The 'rich mixture of objective knowledge, logical deduction and fantasy' that surrounds knowledge might include statements such as: 'society values certain kinds of knowledge over others', 'it is more important to do well at mathematics than art', and 'I was never any good at maths so my child won't be either'. While it is true that 'society values certain kinds of knowledge over others', this apparently objective fact, and the logical deduction that it is therefore particularly important to demonstrate possession and command of that knowledge, masks variation and the fact that such overvaluations are partial and contested. While no one would disagree that it is important to learn mathematics, whether mathematics is *the most important* subject is more debated and other suggestions for top-billing could probably be debated.

Fantasies connected to the primary task of the school are revealed in comments such as 'I was never any good at maths so my child won't be either' or 'his dad is an accountant so it's no surprise he's good at maths'. In each example, the fantasy lies in a suggestion that the ability to take in and reproduce highly valued bodies of knowledge is genetic and/or environmental. Such a defensive move is likely to generate significant levels of stress and anxiety since it deflects attention from the fact that, above all, learning requires work and effort.

Fantasies that conjure up an effortless or magical ability to learn abound: 'If I put the books under my pillow and sleep on them . . .'; '*Really* clever people can do well without effort'; 'You are born good at some subjects and if you are not born like that there is no point trying'. Fantasies such as these cover a desire not to know, not to have to learn. For psychoanalysis, the desire not to know extends into the personal realm. The psychoanalyst Wilfred Bion explains this well. It seemed to him that groups wanted to be able to bypass the difficulty of being with and learning from each other. As teachers, we see this enacted in many ways, not least the belief that a class discussion is not as good, as useful, or as nourishing as being told the answers or fed the curriculum by the teacher. And it was not simply that people do not want to have to talk to and learn from each other:

There is a hatred of having to learn by experience at all, and lack of faith in the worth of such a kind of learning. A little experience of groups soon shows that this is not simply a negative attitude; the process of development is really being compared with some other state, the nature of which is not immediately apparent. The belief in this other state often shows itself in everyday life, perhaps most clearly in the schoolboy belief in the hero who never does any work and yet is always top of the form – the opposite of the 'swot', in fact.

In the group it becomes very clear that this longed-for alternative to the group procedure is really something like arriving fully equipped as an adult fitted by instinct to know without training or development exactly how to live and move and have his being in a group.

(Bion, 1961: 89)

The business of learning is dangerous, not only because it is difficult and challenging and thereby risks failure, but also because of its proximity to love (and therefore also to hate, acceptance and rejection). If love is demonstrated by acts of caring, nurturing, feeding, through acts of kindness and the symbolism of gifts, then teaching, which involves the metaphorical exchange of all these goods, is an act of love. For parents, the concern that their child may love someone more or better than themselves can become an anxiety relating to the primary task of the school. Parental anxieties may be narcissistic and relate to their role as progenitor and primary carer: Have I, by being me, damaged my child? Is my child deficient because I am deficient? Can he or she be successful and happy with me as a parent? Anxieties may also relate to envy of the teacher who is believed to spend more time with the child and who may be felt to be able to give their child something that as parents they cannot (knowledge/learning).

Anxieties such as these might be alleviated by questioning and measuring children. Walkerdine, Lucey and Melody (2001) explore the ways in which the implications of assessment, judgements about success and failure, play out differently for working- and middle-class parents. In this drama, 'normality' is defined by middle-class practices, specifically the practices of middle-class mothers and those middle-class professionals (social workers, health visitors and teachers, who are often also women) who police the boundaries marking working-class (mothering) practices as 'other' and deficient. While patterns of failure were found to be familiar to working-class families, the costs of middle-class success are less frequently told. They describe the differences they found:

It is difficult to overstate the way in which very high academic performance is routinely understood as ordinary and simply the level that is expected [in middle-class families]. Working-class girls who have achieved reasonably good exam results typically receive a lot of praise from their parents, and seemed to take pride in their own achievements. In contrast, middle-class girls, many of whom achieved outstanding exam results . . . found it considerably more difficult to be proud of their performance, or to hold on to a sense of what they had achieved ... believing they were not 'good enough'. Despite the evidence of their grades ... For the middle-class girls, failure was simply not an option: whatever else happened, they were compelled to succeed educationally.

(Walkerdine, Lucey and Melody, 2001: 179–80)

The primary task of the school will be perceived differently by different individuals and from different social and cultural positions. Knowledge and development might be understood and valued differently – for themselves and in relation to each other – by different sections of the community. To assume otherwise is deeply problematic.

As a parent, how would it be to believe that someone else knows better than me what my child needs? The relationship between teaching and love is complicated by real and phantasised relations to food and worthiness (Winnicott, 1964). For children, the experience of having no control over what they are to learn can also be deeply frustrating as they too are subjected to their own 'rich mixture of objective knowledge, logical deduction and fantasy'. Like Bion's adult clients, children hate learning from experience, and entertain magical fantasies that remove the pain of having to learn.

The development of the child

Children occupy a very particular place in society, and recent work in the sociology of childhood has drawn attention to the meanings conveyed by terms such as 'the child', 'childhood' and 'children' (James and James, 2004; Mayall, 2002; Prout, 2005). These terms convey neutral, sexless, degendered, unraced and unclassed generalised and normalised 'children' and in so doing they hide the effects that real social practices have on real, individual children. If we consider even just the titles of recent policy imperatives like 'Every Child Matters' we can ask: Do all children matter equally? Does 'the child' who truants to engage in criminal activity 'matter' as much and in the same ways as 'the child' whose intellectual precociousness startles and delights his (or her?) teachers?

There are many models of childhood which are drawn upon in social life and social policy. For example, children may be seen as the possessions and responsibility of their families, and as such they become private goods rather than public responsibilities. Alternatively, children may be viewed as vulnerable and in need of protection; childhood may be seen as an unproductive, wasteful time; children can be excluded from public spaces and held at the margins of society for their own good, to protect them from dangerous traffic and strangers; and childhood can be viewed as a preparatory phase in which children, as 'human becomings', are somewhat less than human beings (Mayall, 2002; Qvortrup, 2005). Further, as Mayall (2002) has pointed out, middle-class children tend to be valued over working-class children, with middle-class children being regarded as potentially more useful through, for example, their higher earning (tax-paying) potential. This divide in social class and income, which she suggests increased between 1979 and 1997, 'has supported and promoted a culture of victim-blaming, reduced support for families [and], privatised services. The private education system ensures that powerful people such as politicians and the wealthy regard state education as inferior for inferior people' (Mayall, 2002: 165).

The school's role in passively overseeing or actively encouraging child development creates particular fantasies that alleviate adult anxieties relating to our own aggression, toxicity and ignorance. That schools take children in very young, by the age of four in England, and that children are treated as 'innocent' and 'our hope for the future', places huge burdens of responsibility on schools and teachers and on the children themselves. The Enlightenment and Victorian metaphor of the child as a developing flower, beloved of child-centred educators, persists even now. Moss and Penn cite Froebel: 'Man as a child resembles the flower on the plant, the blossom on the tree; as these are in relation to the tree, so is the child in relation to humanity, a young bud, a fresh blossom' (1996: 51). This metaphor summons up particular images: of steady growth, of strong stems, of the outgrowth of leaves and buds, and of the hoped-for flowering or blooming. These all mask concerns about stunted growth, twisted stems, buds nipped by frost and blooms that arrive late or are cut off. Parental concerns that their child is developing as they 'should', that they are keeping up with their peers and making good progress hint at these anxieties. The horticultural metaphor also encourages us to expect the presence of sunshine, gentle rain and good earth in the form of (platonic) love and the wise giving of appropriate tasks and experiences that will feed and stimulate growing minds.

And if the child does 'fail to bloom' who will be held responsible? The parent, the child, the teacher, the school, or someone else? Does it matter which particular child we are talking about?

The overlay of knowledge on the developing child

So education is handed to our 'innocent' children who are in some respects treated as *tabulae rasae*, blank slates, upon which can be written a safe version of history so that previous mistakes will not be repeated, 'good' understandings of the spoken and written word will flourish, enough understanding of culture will enable a coherent community to develop or be sustained. Written out like this there is something faintly ridiculous about these claims. We know children are neither 'innocent' nor empty vessels to be filled; in fact they come into school knowing a lot, perhaps too much of some things. There is a startling contrast between the metaphors of child development and the metaphors of learning: the former implicates innate and apparently natural processes which unfold in a structured and predictable fashion; the latter, the unstructured and culturally driven ('unnatural') inscription of learning on a blank slate. There is, then, a tension at the heart of the way children are constructed under aspects of the primary task of the school.

The splitting evident in divisions of social class and gender is also evident in relation to generation. These different ways of thinking about childhood suggest adult fantasies about themselves and children, not least independent adult omniscience and the dependent status of children. In an interesting exploration of the 'madness of childhood' Chris Jenks explores the conjunction of childhood, read as a state of dependency, and authority, understood as a state of possessing knowledge. He uncovers the way in which the place of childhood is a place of impossibility:

> [Children] are placed in the powerless and strangely disadvantageous situation of always being required to submit to the violence of the existing socio-historical order, but they have not been prewarned. Children 'learn the hard way' which is another way of saying that they consistently, either willingly or unwillingly, flout the norms, rules and conventions of their adults' society. Adults call it learning, maturation or socialisation but, whatever, its outcome is largely predictable. Children explore and exceed limits on a constant basis; indeed, when they cease to behave in this manner they are deemed no longer to be children.
>
> (Jenks, 2005: 122)

This impossible space enables those who are not-children to construct children as variously mad, stupid, evil, lazy, sinful, wilful and suggestible (or their opposites – impossibly good or impossibly bad) and therefore in need of control, supervision and socialisation.

To illustrate this, Jenks reflects on the media handling of the murder of two-year-old James Bulger by two ten-year-olds[2] to think through the way in which notions of demonic children are seen to threaten not only the well-being of 'innocents' but also the stability of civilisation; the adult-collective itself. This fear of children suggests a fear of ourselves, since we were all once young. The association of childhood with innocence, a state of not knowing, may relate to the blankness of our own early memories. The link to demonic evil similarly may be indicative of a fear of what we may once have fantasised; an awareness of our own repressed darknesses. The need to control and overwrite this relatively little-remembered phase of life lends to the task of education an urgency that is reflected in recent debates about failing schools, academic under-achievement and failure, criminality, teenage pregnancy, drug use and bullying. Legislation from the apparently open and positively framed 'Every Child Matters' agenda (DfES, 2004) to the more aggressively reactive Antisocial Behaviour Orders (ASBOs) (The Youth Justice Board, 2006) is provided to enable adults to provide safety through control.

Adult behaviours demonstrate fear but also something of an envy of youth. We envy the slender, supple bodies and lives apparently full of potential which contrast so poignantly with the uncertainty of ageing bodies, serial disappointments and death. Tinges of this envy underpin suggestions that 'education is wasted on the young' and fuel vindictive, punitive tirades against those who turn their backs on knowledge and refuse to do what is good for them. So teachers are handed the job we cannot do: controlling and giving knowledge to children, turning them into responsible adults. In doing this 'we' split children, schools and teachers off from the rest of society, failing to recognise that children, schools and teachers are all also members of the society that would disown them, that they reflect the difficulties of society and are not separate and different from them. Perhaps this is why *we* do not really trust *them* to do the job properly; they fail to be utterly altruistic, are motivated by self-interest, they exploit and corrupt. While teachers might wonder whether they can trust parents to love their children enough (but perhaps not too much) so that they will be able to receive the goodness of school, the public imagination is more exercised by its lack of trust for teachers. How can we trust that the (platonic) love of the teacher will not turn into the more erotic love of the lover (Sikes and Piper, 2010)? The recent case of the (female) nursery worker (Morris, 2009) who abused very young children and took photographs of her abuse for an internet pae-dophile ring has disturbed, once again, the notion of schools as a safe place and, more unusually, of women as safe carers.

The tension here is almost unbearable, and attempts to contain the anxiety gen-erated can be read in the social defences of endless policy interventions – from the need for criminal record bureau (CRB) checks for all adults in contact with schools to the legal requirement for children to be in school. The levels of activity needed to maintain the fantasy of, and defend against, both the danger to civilisation from demonic youth *and* the danger to innocent children from demonic adults diverts us from the mundane normalcy of most life lived and the terror of our own danger-ous fantasies and fantasies of dangerousness.

The internal objects in teachers' inner representational worlds

Teachers, like nurses, are entrusted to look after those who are vulnerable in soci-ety, those who cannot care for themselves, the very young rather than the very ill or injured. A suggestion made by psychoanalysis is that this conjunction, evoking earlier experiences relating to vulnerability and care, creates resonances in the unconscious. Where early contexts and experiences are evoked, we project our unconscious phantasies into current situations, including work situations, and experience what happens around us as both objective reality and phantasy. This process creates the non-rational templates for our beliefs and values as the phan-tasies are poked and prodded by what we perceive to be happening around us and early feelings are re-experienced. Projecting phantasies into objective reality is a psychic defence we all use; it enables us to gain control (or try to gain control) over our anxieties: if our terror is that there will be no one to care for us when we are vulnerable, then by projecting this fear on to others, reading it in the world around us and answering the perceived demand for care, we can try to control and contain or alleviate the anxiety in ourselves. But the process can become unreliable, back-fire and have unintended, negative consequences including, as Menzies Lyth suggests, burn-out among professionals. To make sense of this we need to think about the ways in which unconscious phantasy emerges into the world through the words we choose, the ideas we evoke, the ways our beliefs and values structure our actions. That is, we need to think about the *symbolisations* we draw upon and which are used in our communications with others.

Klein suggests that in the early stages of ego formation, defences against anxiety are aggressive and manifest in destructive impulses – kicking, biting and tearing – responses which she describes as 'sadistic'. At this early stage, we need to accept that the child does not have a full picture of (for example) his mother but is attacking parts of her, retaliating in phantasy more than in reality. For Klein, these early defences are constructed against two sources of perceived danger: the subject's own sadism and the object of his sadistic attack.

> In relation to the subject's own sadism the defence implies expulsion, whereas in relation to the object it implies destruction. The sadism becomes a source of danger because it offers an occasion for the liberation of anxiety and also because the weapons employed to destroy the object are felt by the subject to be levelled at his person also. The object of the attack becomes a source of danger because the subject fears similar, retaliatory attacks from it. Thus, the wholly undeveloped ego is faced with a task which at this stage is quite beyond it – the task of mastering the severest anxiety.
>
> (Klein, 1930: 97)

The infant (for Klein, writing in 1930, a boy but in fact either a boy or a girl) is afraid both that his own powerfully negative feelings will overwhelm him, and that the object of his attacks will take revenge and destroy him. Yet he lacks the levels of symbolisation needed to contain and work through the anxieties. Conceiving of the object requires symbolisation of some kind. As Klein puts it:

> [T]he child's earliest reality is wholly phantastic; he is surrounded with objects of anxiety, and in this respect excrement, organs, objects, things animate and inanimate are to begin with equivalent to one another. As the ego develops, a true relation to reality is gradually established out of this unreal reality. Thus the development of the ego and the relation to reality depend on the degree of the ego's capacity at a very early period to tolerate the pressure of the earliest anxiety situations . . . A sufficient quantity of anxiety is the necessary basis for an abundance of symbol formation and of phantasy; an adequate capacity on the part of the ego to tolerate anxiety is necessary if it is to be satisfactorily worked over and if this basic phase is to have a favourable issue and the development of the ego is to be successful.
>
> (Klein, 1930: 98)

Our capacity for symbolisation is an important part of the way in which we understand ourselves as human. Symbolisation is the capacity to attach symbols – words and images – to experiences. Psychoanalytically, that means it is one of the ways in which unconscious phantasy emerges into the world. Importantly, the labels we learn to attach to experiences never entirely capture the whole experience. And, of course, our experiences shift and change all the time, and one person's experiences will never be exactly the same as another's. Even an apparently simple idea-word like 'dog' can cause difficulties, although to operate in the world we behave as if communication involved the unproblematic passing of meaning from speaker to listener; as if we all understand 'dog' in the same way. In reality, while we may be able to agree on some basic qualities – four legs, a tail, barks and so forth – the prototypical 'dog' we carry around will vary. If 'dog' for me is a puppy dozing fluffily in a patch of sunlight, the word and the thing will evoke a different response in me than if 'dog' is a terrifying toothsome guard dog snarling at the end of its chain. If that variation is true for something as apparently concrete as a dog, what about abstract ideas like love, hate, anger and envy? This also suggests that all symbolisation comes with flows of affect which we may or may not be aware of, but which will colour our meanings and understandings in communication.

Through an analysis of play, the gradual learning of words and shifting attributions of meanings to words and actions, Klein (1930) explored the role of symbolisation in the development of the ego. Her conclusions were that we need to experience anxiety to learn, that it is the experience of tolerable levels of anxiety that enables us to form symbols. If I can experience what is happening to me, then I can engage with someone else and learn to attach a word to what I experience. If the anxiety provoked by the experience is too great, or if we shut off from it completely, then no symbol formation is possible and learning cannot take place. Unconscious anxiety is experienced as a tension; this is eased by phantasy and expressed through symbolisation. The act of symbolisation enables the anxiety to be contained and controlled. There needs to be an itch to scratch – enough of an itch to notice, and in a place where the skin is not so raw that scratching is unbearable. Extending the metaphor, this itch, the anxiety and the tension it generates, the desire to scratch, is what enables us to learn. Klein calls this the *epistemophilic impulse*: an impulse towards knowledge. Chapter 7 will explore Klein's and Bion's development of these ideas in greater detail.

Using Klein's ideas, Menzies Lyth noted the way in which the nurses and patients in her study tended to confuse the object and the symbol. She noted that a 'close resemblance of the phantasy and objective situations in nursing constitutes a threat that symbolic representation will degenerate into symbolic equation' (Menzies Lyth, 1960: 165). That is, there is a close and evocative relationship between the experience of having been taken care of as a vulnerable infant and taking care of someone else who is vulnerable. This observation is also true of teaching although the perspective is somewhat different since the primary tasks of the two institutions (the hospital and the school) are different.

A hypothetical example may help to make this less abstract and bring it back to education. As an adult, the anxieties I had as a child that I would not be worthy of love and acceptance may lead me to continue to seek the approval and love of authorities. One way I symbolise this is by taking to myself the approval I was given as a child: I am a good girl. Or at least, when I am a good girl I imagine I receive the love I crave; the symbol 'good girl' contains and soothes my anxieties that I am unlovable. Education, in putting us at the mercy of quasi-parental figures (teachers are after all *in loco parentis*), puts me back in touch with anxieties about whether or not my parents really love me, whether they will reliably look after me, etc. Now, as a student an essay I have handed in has been marked as a fail. The distinction being made is between *I failed* and *the essay failed*. If in phantasy I experience my academic outputs as identical with myself (through symbolic equation) rather than as representative of my efforts (through symbolic representation), the failure of the academic output becomes a personal failure.

In this example, the way the phantasy association between my academic output and my self works to reduce anxiety might be that I like my tutor, I imagine she likes me so she will like my essay, I am a good girl so my essay is a good essay. This association, this symbolisation, makes the anxiety of producing an essay, of exposing myself to judgement, marginally more bearable. However, if I fail, the sense of danger and exposure is elevated, the symbolisation has worked in reverse and anxiety has been increased. This makes sense only if we acknowledge the way in which the organisational structure of education puts me back into a familial context and recalls and replays phantasies that emerged to enable me to live in that setting.

From a Kleinian perspective, it is through these mechanisms that the phantasies provoked by the primary task (overlaying some notion of development with the transmission of knowledge) are evoked: the similarities prompted by the affects called up by the symbolisation of words, ideas and deeds. It is in our capacity (or otherwise) to know and hold as different the symbol and the object that our ability to continue to usefully symbolise, contain and alleviate anxieties rests.

The social defences of the school

For Menzies Lyth, members of the institution 'use' the organisation to put in place the means to avoid anxiety. She describes the anxieties likely to be provoked by a close relationship with a very ill person and the way these are managed by fragmenting patient care so that such relationships cannot develop. Once again, however, the defences of the hospital are not the defences of the school; they may be similar but they need rethinking.

The major systems of education relate to both aspects of its primary task. In relation to knowledge, the curriculum and assessment are paramount, while in relation to the developing learner, the organisation of classes into age groups and expectations of behaviour, particularly compliance, seem key. For Alan Bass 'wherever one finds systematicity, one can, from a psychoanalytic point of view, ask the question of what unbearable piece of reality is being defended against by means of the system' (Bass, 1998: 426). This claim, that all the systems and routines we put in place are plasters that cover over something we cannot look at, is uncomfortable. After all, we put a lot of effort into the creation and management of these systems (and defences do serve a purpose). However, for educators, Bion's suggestion that defences are defences against thinking may be even more unpalatable – our business as teachers is apparently the development and encouragement of thinking, so why would we put in place defences to stop us doing this? Three modes of being are considered as mechanisms by which social defences are activated: compliance, systematicity and fragmentation.

Compliance

Many policies are put in place to ensure compliance. Britzman (2003) selects the case of 'zero tolerance' policies to illustrate Bion's claim that such a defence is against thinking. She explains that in refusing to tolerate non-compliant behaviour so completely, we are refusing to think about what it might mean for the 'naughty child', other children, or for ourselves. In doing this the phrase, language itself, is stripped of meaning and cannot be thought about:

> Zero-tolerance policies foreclose the capacity for symbolisation and metaphorical knowledge . . . [And] when symbolisation cannot be thought, the symbol no longer *represents* the object, instead it *becomes* the object. When this occurs, perceptions of the world become more and more literal and aggressive, and the capacity for thinkers to think is attacked.
>
> (Britzman, 2003: 114, emphasis in the original)

Despite this danger, control and ensuring that children do in fact learn are central to the teaching enterprise. The disciplining of minds and bodies is fundamental to the work of the teacher, and complaints that the job has become little more than a policing exercise are common. But the need to control, to hold tightly, to clutch, restrain and shape suggests a level of aggression:

> The fantasies of loss of control that haunt student teachers and perhaps all teachers hold in fact very powerful aggressive impulses that are defended against by fantasies of loving and sacrificing for the students . . . [H]igher standards and high-stakes testing, corporal punishment, tough-love, the end of social promotion, and the end of affirmative action, all these offer opportunities for teachers to enjoy their own aggression in the name of the greater good and actually, in some cases, to have the double enjoyment of turning such aggression into a sacrifice: 'This hurts me more than it hurts you', as the punishment is meted out.
>
> (Taubman, 2006: 30)

Taubman suggests we need to be as suspicious and wary of protestations of love and self-sacrifice as we are of overt anger and violence; they are two sides of the same coin. This terrifying suggestion is actively denied by social fantasies of the caring and nurturing teacher. The valorisation of compliance, love and 'good' behaviour make it difficult to think constructively about subversion and resistance although, as I will suggest in chapter 4, these might usefully be read as creative responses to the classroom.

Systematicity

The codification of knowledge into a formal curriculum enables us to behave as if knowledge were certain and fixed, as if knowledge that is important can be separated from less important knowledge, and as if all knowledge is desirable. Assessment procedures enable us to behave as if knowledge were measurable, as if teaching and knowing were directly and unproblematically related, as if what is known can be directly accessed. Anxieties that knowledge might be shifting and uncertain, that coming to know might be a stuttering process rather than a clean, one-off event, not knowing what or how we know anything, fears of forgetting, not knowing, and the sense that teaching's relation to learning might be problematic, are all alleviated by the presence of the curriculum and assessment procedures.

These procedures also enable us to differentiate the worthy student from the unworthy one. We make this distinction in many ways. Jenny Shaw's (1995) exploration in *Education, Gender and Anxiety* looks at some of the ways in which teachers' status as *in loco parentis* imports gender into the endeavour – whether as the 'harsh' father or the 'nurturing' mother – and problematises both boys' and girls' relations to schooling, knowledge and learning. But other identifiable qualities of the learner are also used to sort and classify students: social class, 'race', well-ness or 'disability', and geographical location. Powell and Barber focus on the relief the notion of the urban school provides:

> The 'institution in the mind' of school requires a denigrated 'other', someone to do badly, someone to fail, and someone to be less capable. The unconscious sorting and ranking function of education leaves each of us needing a 'home' for our incompetence, and urban education has taken that role. [. . .] Any analysis of urban education that focusses on the immediate players, however, blames the victims for their fate in a system designed to assure their failure. It simultaneously relieves us from examining how we psychically (and potentially materially) benefit from our complicity in its operation. Revitalising the primary task of providing authentic teaching and learning for urban children would have to include some opportunity for them to make sense of why they find themselves in their circumstances, and to make meaning out of their own lives. Any curriculum that grapples with those larger

questions such as race, poverty, homelessness, gender and so forth, begins to indict the larger citizenry, our culture, and us. If we question why urban children are relegated to the weakest, poorest performing parts of the system . . . then we make ourselves vulnerable to the exploration of how we have 'earned' our positions of privilege.

(Powell and Barber, 2006: 47)

In a place that idealises rationality, learning and knowing, what can we do with our affect, our non-rational parts, with our failures, our hatred of learning and with our refusals to know?

Fragmentation

Fragmentation is another powerful social defence. In schools it fulfils several tasks similar to those identified by Menzies Lyth, including the splitting up of caring relationships and 'depersonalisation, categorisation and denial of the significance of the individual' (1960: 166). The creation of cohorts, the gathering together and categorisation of learners by age (literal in compulsory schooling, metaphorical in post-compulsory education), is a significant systemisation of the developmental aspect of teaching. The passing of the learner from one teacher to the next, whether within the day or annually, acts to 'inhibit the full person-to-person relationship' (Menzies Lyth, 1960: 166). We are encouraged to believe that whichever teacher teaches us, the nature and 'quality' of what we get will be equivalent. Despite this assurance, experience teaches us that this is not so: the nature of what is learned is highly dependent on the experience of the pedagogic relationship (Bibby, 2009b). And getting too close to children can be problematic for teachers, perhaps especially for the teachers of very young children. Yet we continue to gather them under the care of one teacher for a whole year. What does the maintenance of close relationships with the younger children signal about our anxieties in the early years, and how do these translate across into the early years of other pedagogic relationships?

Even within the intimacies that exist, relationships are split up. To support and institutionalise this, we refuse to acknowledge the losses and bereavements that interrupt learning and teaching lives. There are the small, frequent losses rendered invisible by routines: the ends of lessons and days, and those that slide past as we let go of the 'me that doesn't understand this' and embrace the new 'me that does (understand this)'. Larger losses associated with the ends of academic years and the move between teachers and schools are more difficult to ignore. For these, there are small rituals, the giving of awards or cards and gifts; but the significance of the loss is often overlooked in the desire to be forward-looking. At the end of each stage of schooling, the sadness of the loss of a phase of life and long friendships, of achievements and disappointments, is avoided by an overwhelming focus on the future, on growing up and moving on.

Like other institutions, schools appear to fear that familiarity will breed contempt and that respect can exist only inside formal relationships. So formality and role definitions are used to create 'professional' distance. Naming teachers 'Miss Jones' or 'Mr Smith' rather than Amanda or Andy, the use of 'dinner ladies' and teaching assistants to take on some of the pastoral roles, and the strict demarcation of work and play are organisational tropes that enable some separation of the parental and quasi-parental roles.

What anxieties do these defences protect against, what phantasies do they symbolise? And, given the energy and effort that go into developing and working with these systems, how can Bion say that they are ways by which we enable ourselves not to think? These are some of the questions that are looked at in the chapters to come.

Moving forwards

This chapter has considered the primary task of the school. In the title this suggestion is followed by a question mark, a device used to signal the impossibility of deciding what a primary task might be. Under an accountability lens the primary task might be to attract pupils and other funding streams to ensure the survival of the institution. Or, as Powell and Barber suggest, the school's primary task might be its sorting and ranking function. However one conceives the task, fantasies will emerge and these will act as defences or force the emergence of defences.

For the purposes of this chapter the primary task was assumed to have two dimensions: the development of the child, and the creation, control and transmission of knowledge. The work of teaching, learning and parenting all arouse strong and conflicting feelings: love, resentment, hate, aggression and gratitude. By affording some protection from the difficulties of dependence and vulnerability (our own and that of others), and situations, events, tasks, activities and relationships that evoke anxiety, compliance, systematicity and fragmentation were identified as mechanisms of institutional defence. But, as these mechanisms protect, so they generate new difficulties. As Deborah Britzman notes: 'Habits of avoidance – inhibitions of curiosity – are cultivated in education as a defence against its structures of authority, dependency, and interference. And these strategies, affected by what they defend against, also preserve the anxiety of learning' (2003: 4).

So, for example, we codify knowledge and then fragment the curriculum to tame and control the sheer weight of what could be selected to present to learners. By creating lists of important knowledge we soothe ourselves into believing that wise choices have been made, nothing important will be forgotten. But soothing, covering over a phantasy or anxiety, does not make it go away. Indeed, denying the terror and difficulty of the thing we seek to defend against reaffirms its troublesome importance. The curriculum lists the knowledge but the knowledge not on the list keeps intruding; the elephant does not leave the room. We insist that we need only teach what is on the curriculum; compliance to the policy demand enables us to shuffle difficult knowledge off for someone else to teach.

We normalise child development and assign 'appropriate' knowledge to different groups so we don't either 'starve' them of what they deserve or 'choke them' with ideas that are too difficult, too 'grown up'; but events in the real world intrude. We decide that the reception class is too young to discuss the latest terrorist outrage and the accompanying religious tensions. But the children are part of those tensions, out there, in the world, in their home communities. And we can test the children to make sure the knowledge has 'gone in'. If we do this at the end of the year, then any 'blame' for what has not been learned can be placed on children who are lazy or stupid (although we take credit where there is success) and the problem of remediation is passed on to the next teacher (assuming that whatever was not learned is still on the curriculum). The rational processes, fantasies, anxieties and defences intertwine in a complex dance of creation and destruction, compliance and resistance, influence and rejection.

An important issue raised by any discussion of the primary task of the school is that we recognise the impossibility of the demand that we fulfil the task, and the necessity that we keep trying anyway. The need to learn is not confined to the young, the job of learning does not end at the school gates, the children we conveniently think of as needing our (adult) care and love/teaching are no different from us. Their resistances to learning and desires not to know are ours; we share their wish to know without the troublesome process of coming to know; aggressive impulses do not belong only to the un(der)civilised young. While we might want to separate out 'teachers' and 'learners' and to occupy one position or the other, the positions are fluid and interchangeable. Accepting this, knowing that we can learn important things from and with those we teach, requires humility and a willingness to listen. Knowing and accepting our responsibilities while maintaining a willingness to listen is a very difficult balance to find. Finding some balance will require constant effort to hold the tension aroused by our anxieties. We need to embrace the hard and ceaseless work of recognising compliance, fragmentation and systematicity for what they are and thinking past their pragmatic functions to the psychoanalytic functions.

3   Mirror, mirror on the wall
The Lacanian mirror in the classroom

In the first Harry Potter book (Rowling, 1998), the eponymous hero discovers a magical room containing the Mirror of Erised. Carved around the top of the mirror's ornate frame are the words 'Erised stra ehru oyt ube cafru oyt on wohsi'. The mirror shows *not your face but your heart's desire*. The pain of this mirror and its representations, as well as its seductive power, take some time to become clear, and in a distressing episode Harry and his friend Ron are overwhelmed with greed and disappointment when it becomes evident that each cannot see the other's image (they cannot know the other's dream). The headmaster, Dumbledore, explains to Harry:

> [The mirror] shows us nothing more or less than the deepest, most desperate desire of our hearts. You, who have never known your family, see them standing around you. Ronald Weasley, who has always been overshadowed by his brothers, sees himself standing alone, the best of all of them. However, this mirror will give us neither knowledge or truth. Men have wasted away before it, entranced by what they have seen, or been driven mad, not knowing if what it shows is real or even possible.
>
> (Rowling, 1998: 157)

In showing Harry an image of himself as he would like to be seen, the actions of the magical mirror disrupt our notion of what non-magical mirrors do, offering possibilities for thinking about more 'metaphorical' mirrors. Metaphorical mirrors in education, the mirroring functions of teachers and teaching tools such as assessments, and the processes of identification that make these so powerful, disrupt rational stories about the neutral, benign or positive functions of teachers and assessments. The mirroring we receive, the 'gift' of the assessment, whether complimentary or not, requires we accommodate it, that we find somewhere in ourselves to put it. Of all the mirrors held up to us, which 'reflections' do we most easily recognise and identify with?

This chapter explores what has been described as the mirror metaphor in psychoanalysis and uses it as a way to investigate some of the consequences of the small judgements that occur from moment to moment in the classroom. How many learners have a Dumbledore on hand to help them make sense of, and accommodate, the images of themselves they are presented in the classroom? How can the judgements of others come to matter so much to us? Why do they impact upon our identities so strongly? To answer these and other similar questions we need to consider the psychoanalytic process of 'identification' which in turn requires a step back to consider the baby's introduction to life and the metaphorical mirrors of psychoanalysis.

The mirror in psychoanalysis

All psychoanalytic theories begin by positing a newborn baby that can draw no distinction between itself and its mother.[1] It exists in a state of omnipotence believing that it controls the satisfaction of its needs and that all 'external' objects are part of itself:

> For many months, the child remains physiologically incapable of controlling its bodily movement and behaviour . . . its body is an uncoordinated *aggregate*, a series of parts, zones, organs, sensations, needs, and impulses rather than an integrated totality. Each part strives for its own satisfaction with no concern for the body as a whole. It has no experience of corporeal or psychical unity or of occupying a stable position within a corporeally delimited space.
>
> (Grosz, 1990: 33–34, emphasis in the original)

A paradoxical suggestion is that at this stage, *phantasy is reality*, that what the child phantasises is all it knows and so that this is what is 'real' to it. The way in which this phantasised state of unity is described and, most particularly, the way it is believed to be broken and to develop, varies according to different schools of thought. Lacan (2001) uses what he calls 'the mirror stage' to describe the process by which the mind becomes split between a conscious ego and an unconscious.

In the mirror stage, through recognition that it is separate from its (m)other, and that she is beyond its control, the child comes to see itself as something whole and bounded, a unified being who can control its limbs; it comes to recognise a 'me' separate and different from the surrounding 'not me'. This, Lacan suggests, is a process, an act of learning that takes time. Children first introduced to mirrors touch the mirror expecting the image to *be* the person reflected; they must learn that the people who are reflected include themselves and the objects that surround them (they must learn to distinguish between the 'me' and the 'not me'). Returning to Harry Potter in front of the Mirror of Erised, Rowling powerfully evokes the strangeness of this moment by putting Harry (in his invisibility cloak) in front of the magical mirror:

He had to clap his hand to his mouth to stop himself screaming. He whirled around. His heart was pounding . . . for he had seen not only himself in the mirror, but a whole crowd of people standing right behind him. But the room was empty. Breathing very fast, he turned slowly back to the mirror.

There he was, reflected in it, white and scared looking, and there, reflected behind him, were at least ten others . . . They just looked at him smiling. And slowly, Harry looked into the faces of the other people in the mirror and saw other pairs of green eyes like his, other noses like his, even a little old man who looked as if he had Harry's knobbly knees – Harry was looking at his family, for the first time in his life. The Potters smiled and waved at Harry and he stared hungrily back at them, his hands pressed flat against the glass as though he was hoping to fall right through it and reach them.

(Rowling, 1998: 153)

Through careful looking Harry recognises aspects of himself in the others and comes to know that they 'belong' to him, and he to them. For Harry, it took a while to register that the others were his family, but for a real baby encountering a mirror for the first time, it is probably easier to recognise the image belonging to 'not me' which they will have seen before. It is the image that is 'me' that they must learn to distinguish. What seems important in the previous extract is the sense of shock that might accompany seeing something so unexpected and for that sense of recognition to be so desired.

Lacan's mirror stage is described as taking place in front of a real mirror, enabling us to imagine an infant, confronted with this strange and bounded series of beings, issued with a challenge to make sense of what it is seeing. The psychoanalyst Donald Winnicott (1971) extended Lacan's mirror stage back in time to suggest that a child's first mirror lies in its mother's face. In offering the child its expression back to it, the mother mirrors (her interpretation of) its internal state through her smiles, looks of surprise, frowns and sounds. What is important is that the mirror stage suggests a mechanism by which we come to recognise and make sense of our selves by looking to others for the mirror-functions they provide.

Another important aspect of the image in the mirror is that while the child sees itself outside its body (in the mirror) it is simultaneously located in a body it can feel and experience. This double movement contains two processes: alienation and misrecognition. The fact that 'this is me' can be achieved by pointing to the mirror *and* to oneself is characterised as *alienation*. Being able to experience my body corporeally and visually existing in two distinct places leaves open the question: Which is the real me? Simultaneously, having experienced itself as fragmented, 'a series of parts, zones . . . sensations and needs', the image of unity presented in the mirror is a *misrecognition* of ourselves; despite appearances, we remain fundamentally split and fragmented.

The child sees itself as a unified totality . . . in the mirror: it experiences itself in a schism, as a site of fragmentation. The child's identification with its specular image impels it nostalgically to seek out a past symbiotic completeness, even if such a state never existed and is retrospectively imposed on the pre-mirror phase; and to seek an anticipatory or desired (ideal or future) identity in the coherence of the totalised specular image. Lacan claims that the child is now enmeshed in a system of confused recognition/misrecognition: it sees an image of itself that is both accurate (since it is an inverted reflection, the presence of light rays emanating from the child: the image as icon); as well as delusory (since the image prefigured a unity and mastery that the child still lacks). It is the dual, ambivalent relation to its own image that is central to Lacan's account of subjectivity.

(Grosz, 1990: 39)

So we come to desire both a sense of belonging and wholeness, a magical place of *symbiotic completeness* with someone who can know and meet our needs without us having to take the trouble to know and articulate them, without us having to ask and risk rejection, a place where there is no need to face the terrifying uncertainty of our vulnerability; and a coherent, singular and unified identity to match the promise held up by the mirror, an ego ideal – 'the image of the ego, derived from others, which the ego strives to achieve or live up to' (Grosz, 1990: 48). For Lacan, desire is generated in the gap between 'me' as I experience myself (including what I see mirrored by other people) and the 'me' I would like to experience. Desire is, in part, the urge to fill or close that gap.

   This taking up of what we see out there (in the mirror of people's responses to us) is a process called *identification* and it is a key way in which psychoanalytic theories suggest what is 'out there' comes to be 'in here'. Stephen Frosh (2002) discusses the Lacanian notion of identification and the development of the ego. He quotes Lacan as describing the ego as 'the sum of identifications', a layering, a 'superimposition of various coats borrowed from what I will call the bric-à-brac of its props department' (cited in Frosh, 2002: 60). Frosh continues:

The ego is here described as 'the sum of identifications of the subject'. Identification, psychoanalysis attests, is that process whereby the ego takes the object and makes it *subject*, incorporating each object as part of itself. According to Lacan, this is indeed a formative process, but its effect is specifically to create a kind of radical misperception, in which the ego is taken to be the 'truth' of the person when it is actually just 'bric-à-brac', made up of bits and pieces latched onto from outside. Hence there is a sense in which identification *falsifies*, with the subject 'using' the object to sustain a fantasy of integrity of the self . . . Identification, therefore, may well be a major mechanism through which what is outside comes to be registered within, but this also makes it a mode of alienation, whereby the human subject is made a stranger to itself.

(Frosh, 2002: 61, emphasis in the original)

So the ego, the 'I', our sense of self, is made up of a layering of identifications (and disidentifications) we have unconsciously made with objects we have found or been presented with 'out there'. This idea that we are subject to the images provided by specific other people and generalised 'other people' (society, culture) is known as 'the gaze'. This is not the experience of being looked at by someone else, where the looking is assumed to be neutral or passive, 'it is not the gaze of an other; it is the Other's gaze. It is the result of being located in the field of the Other' (Grosz, 1990: 80). That is to say, the gaze is an ideologically loaded system of judgements that frame how we come to be seen and known. The Other (with a capital 'O') is not a person but a place, a location in language and culture, the one who we are subject to. If a teacher judges us to be not achieving a high enough level in our tests, not only is that teacher saying we are not measuring up, but so is the system of judgements her[2] role embodies. And her role is never single: she is teacher but also bearer of adult femininity, she carries some parental functions and is 'expert' in the thing being failed in; she is classed, 'raced' and gendered. As such, she is culturally, historically and professionally located. The teacher/mirror is always tinged, coloured, shaped by her multiple positions. Her judgements and assessments splinter and refract, shattering and scattering the images.

How do assessments add to the layers of coats that children (we all) put on, and how do they impact their (our) sense of self? To answer this question, we need to accept that our most fundamental desire is for a secure identity, to know who we are and to feel that who we feel ourselves to be is seen, recognised and valued by those who are important to us: family, friends and teachers. A secure identity therefore implies that we feel valued and acknowledged. We look for evidence that we are seen and that the way we are seen accords with the way we like to think we are seen; some sense of security is achieved if the gap is not too big.

Lacan's suggestion is that we achieve this by looking to the reaction of those around us to see if we are recognised, to see if our feelings resonate with the feelings in the room. Discussing this process, Mark Bracher draws attention to the way in which physical appearance and ideas are at least as powerful as more overt notions of 'the good student' in forming identities in school. He describes the way emotional mirroring is sought, highlighting our attendance at places we know we will 'fit in': sporting events, concerts, political rallies and so on. But it is never simple:

> A desire for emotional mirroring can be educationally productive, as when the enthusiastic desire of a teacher or student for a particular educational activity or subject matter elicits a similar desire in others in the class. It can also be problematic, as when the enthusiastic desire of the teacher or the majority

deprives some students of the opportunity to voice, or even experience, their own desires. And the desire for emotional mirroring can also be counterproductive for learning and growth when it functions as an obstacle to thinking and reflecting about an issue.

(Bracher, 2002: 103)

So, turning to the material world, what is held up by teachers and how is this received? Do children experience themselves as seen, valued and acknowledged? How and where do they look for value and acknowledgement? What mirroring goes on in the classroom? For the purposes of this chapter, the focus is on mirroring as it is related to academic or learner identities. These are considered apart from gendered, classed and other identities although we need to remember that this separation is artificial, and that they combine and interact in complex ways.

Mirror, mirror on the (classroom) wall, who am I?

A strictly Lacanian use of the metaphor suggests that the mirror is created by the act of looking and that what is seen is entirely a fiction generated by the viewer's desire; this strict interpretation seems to me to absolve the 'mirror' of all responsibility for what is seen. I feel this to be problematic in the context of the classroom so, in what follows, I use the metaphor more flexibly.

When I look in the mirror there are many things that can happen. I can see myself and be more or less happy with what I see. If the mirror has some flaw, I may appear distorted, as in a fairground mirror, or I may see multiple images if the mirror is cracked or faceted. Whether I can use the reflection in the mirror depends on why I am looking in it; if I want to assess a new outfit, a tiny vanity mirror is little help. While all images will be partial and distorted, the ways I 'receive' mirroring from those around me will depend on many things. 'Good' mirroring enables us to use the reflection. While it holds up only a fragment of what might be seen, it is helpful, constructive even, so that if we do not like what we see it is at least presented in a tolerable way or in a supportive environment. 'Bad' mirroring on the other hand is destructive, it gives us images of ourselves that we might want to reject or have no way of understanding. But rejection may not be easy or possible, especially if we do not realise the mirroring is destructive, if we have no opportunity to check what we see or if there is no one to help us think about the image presented. In terms of our identities, key questions include: 'Am I seen?' And if I am, 'How am I seen?' Or perhaps 'Can I be less visible?' And if I am not seen, 'How can I make myself more visible?'

In this section I will draw on data to consider different kinds of mirroring in an academic setting. The difficulty of being and making yourself available for judgement was brought home early in year 5 to one girl, Minnie. While she worked on a drawing, Minnie talked to a researcher (AH):

AH: Why do you keep rubbing your picture out?
Minnie: Because I want it to be perfect.
AH: Why do you want it to be perfect?
Minnie: Because *I* want to be perfect.
AH: And how will you know it's perfect?
Minnie: When everyone likes it.
AH: And what if there's one person who doesn't like it?
Minnie: It's not perfect.

Here, Minnie is trying (and failing) to occupy a place of perfection. The difficulty is that she is conflating her drawing with herself. This act is a violent one, simplifying and reducing herself, chopping away sides of her self and whittling away her complexities. The drawing, a two-dimensional representation of a scene from a story, can never contain all that she is, but her experience of vulnerability to criticism is made vivid by the analogy she draws. The constant sense of exposure, combined with the constant need for reassurance that one is seen, valued and can be acknowledged, that one is good enough and therefore deserving of notice (love), make the classroom a very complex and potentially dangerous place, one that generates stress for all involved. A year later, in year 6, Minnie and her friend Rani were still struggling with the difficult demand of impossible perfection. In this extract they are talking to another researcher (SC):

SC: Why do you think the teachers get so stressed?
Minnie: Because they want it to be perfect.
Rani: Yes, it all has to be perfect.
Minnie: They think we are perfect child, but we are not. We are just children.
Rani: Yeah, every child ain't perfect. There is always something . . .
Minnie: [Interrupts] Wrong with them.
Rani: Not wrong with them. But they ask that we all be perfect.

There is an important difference in Rani and Minnie's notions of perfection. For Minnie, being imperfect means there is something wrong, and perhaps she feels guilt at a flaw she senses but cannot name or resolve. For Rani, imperfection is simpler, an absence of perfection, and carries no kernel of wrongness – a position that would be easier to live with.

The fear of (im)perfection can bring paranoia, an assumption that the good is not visible and that only the 'bad' will be noticed. This fear is common and was expressed several times by different children in the fieldwork undertaken. During year 6, towards the end of our research, Rani went to great lengths to explain her fantasy that teachers talk about children in the staffroom. She felt that they shared information in a distorted way and that other teachers therefore become prejudiced about her work and, by extension, her. For her, the 'goodness' and 'badness' of work became a reflection of her as a person:

TB: Maybe it's a good thing? Maybe they're saying good things about you?

Rani: But I've just done bad things so how can they? Sometimes they do say good things like 'Oh I'm impressed with Rani for doing her art' and then she might say 'Oh I'm impressed with her vocabulary' and all that but then they – they're not just going to say a good part, they're also going to say about a bad part. But I don't know. And not just around me – it's around other children as well. But that's my opinion, I don't like it. Other children might like it . . . [but] I don't think it's fair.

She went on to explain that no one likes being talked about behind their back. At this point, we were interrupted by two of Rani's friends who came to say that playtime was over and the class was coming back. While Yasmin held back and spoke from the door, Sophie came right in, stamped her feet and asked, in a very demanding and accusing way: 'What are you doing in here? You're talking about us! About me! Maths time now!' Sophie's paranoia nicely punctured the conversation we had been having and, once Sophie had gone, enabled us to look at the phenomena and share a wry laugh about our own paranoia and fear of misrepresentation. There is a terrible ambivalence and tension around being seen – wanting to be recognised, valued and acknowledged but knowing that visibility can also bring misrecognition, contempt and dismissal. It is to these different kinds of experience that we now turn.

'Good' mirroring

Our field notes recorded very few examples of children giving evidence of feeling seen, valued and acknowledged. This does not mean that it did not happen, but any manifestations passed unnoticed. In Grafton School, it was remarkably rare for a teacher to give an individual specific positive feedback, and when it happened it tended to take place in complex circumstances that might have muddied the message. For example, during a year 5 English lesson Miss Middleton was moving very fast through a series of closed questions and one-word answers. The pace she maintained was such that Mohammed was unable to keep up. Desperate to answer anything, eventually he simply put his hand up and left it up; despite this he still did not get chosen. The anger he felt at the impossibility of keeping up and his failure to be seen was evidenced by his muttered 'Hello! You bitch' as she finished that phase of the lesson. Shortly after this, though, the picture changed. Miss Middleton had, she told them, read their stories and was impressed by Mohammed's: 'It was the best writing I've seen from you all year, I knew you had it in you,' she told him. He looked happy and smiled to himself. Perhaps it was a relief to experience himself as transparent, so that what was hidden inside could be seen (I knew you had it in you). Is it possible that the moment of glory wiped out the minutes of agony and anger? Or did it only overlay them? We cannot know, and Mohammed probably could not tell us either. The difficult, if unanswerable, question is: Does it matter?

Like most of the positive mirroring we observed, Mohammed's moment in the sun passed quickly and no response from him was observed other than his smile. Only one more vocal response was noted and, as with Mohammed's complaint, if the researcher had not been sitting next to Katie, it would have been missed:

> Katie asks if she has to copy what is written on the board. Miss Warner tells her 'You use them to help you. I think you're too clever to need to copy it, Katie.' Katie looks *very* pleased with this compliment and says *sotto voce*: 'I am, I am.'

> (field notes)

Katie was evidently delighted to have her undoubted cleverness recognised in this way, but she felt the need to mute her pleasure and its celebration. This stands in marked contrast to the many loud, triumphant cries of 'yes!' that would erupt when tests were being self-marked communally. These yelps of delight seemed to be for public consumption, telling peers and the teacher that they were pleased with themselves. These staged performances of success, however, often seemed designed as much to cover up disappointment and moments of vulnerability. But why would Katie feel the need to hide her celebration? This question and themes of perfection and envy are explored in more detail in chapter 5.

More problematic mirroring

Most mirroring is ambivalent. It has the potential to be used constructively if it can be thought about, although the time, space and help to think are not always made available. Not only is the help rarely there but the public nature of a comment can add to the difficulty of living with the experience (Bibby, 2002). Typically, when problematic stories of classroom life are shared, people rightly deplore the teacher's actions and wonder how the child might have *felt* (although feelings are often quite evidently negative). It might be more instructive to ask how a child might 'read' her or himself in such a situation, and what image of themselves they see reflected in the teacher's words and actions.

Negative mirroring and humiliation

The two examples here came from one lesson in year 6. The level of sarcasm and humiliation meted out was unusual but not unique. The class had been given a short test and was working through the answers together. The teacher, Mrs Norton, seemed annoyed, although why was not clear. She pursued children for answers, seeming unconcerned about how she got them. After a series of apparently frustrating exchanges she asked Muhi how many 5 ps there are in a pound.

He did not know. At this point, rather than offering hints, guidance or encouragement, she asked a series of sarcastic questions that seemed geared at making Muhi feel foolish:

Mrs Norton: How many 5 ps make a pound?
Muhi: I don't know.
Mrs N: Muhi, do you know anything about money?
Muhi: [no response, others giggle]
Mrs N: Do you go to the shops? [no response] Have you seen a 2 p coin?
                     Have you seen a 5 p coin?

By this point, Muhi just seemed confused and much more worried about his derided position than getting the answer. Finally he was rescued when some of the other children blurted out 'twenty' and, at Mrs Norton's insistence, he was able to repeat this. We cannot know how Muhi understood himself at this moment or subsequently as a response to this moment. Indeed, he may have repressed the episode. But repression is not erasure; it becomes part of the unconscious and continues to circulate in phantasies, fantasies and desires. He was certainly being shown an image of himself as stupid and contemptible; an impoverished version of himself that was made visible to him *and* the rest of the class. There was poverty of factual knowledge (ignorance), poverty of cultural knowledge (one who does not know England, the new immigrant),[3] poverty of age, responsibility and masculinity (infantilised as a 'mummy's-boy', overprotected and not allowed to go out alone). As an observer I found her apparent contempt for him shocking, the implications of her words infuriating. For the rest of the class, there must also have been a fear that this could happen to them and a fear that this impoverished story might also be theirs: Am I like that?

Once all the questions had been gone through, Mrs Norton asked: 'Who got 20 out of 20?' No one had. But Shanhrul was so excited about his mark that he blurted out 'I got 19!' He was not going to be allowed his pleasure, though, and Mrs Norton replied: 'Well I'm not going to read yours now' and she moved on to 18 and 17 leaving Shanhrul looking dejected. When she got to 15 she changed the question: 'Who got 15 and over?' Shanhrul did not put up his hand. He probably was not listening by then, but she reprimanded him again: 'Shanhrul! You got 15 and over didn't you? *15 or more*?!' But nothing could re-inspire his earlier excitement. Indeed, his 'clever' moment has been turned into a 'stupid' one, celebration to jeering.

Winnicott, in discussing the psychotherapist's mirroring role, cautions against premature mirroring, of giving back to the patient more than they can manage at any particular time: 'premature interpretation . . . annihilates the creativity of the patient and is traumatic in the sense of being against the maturational process' (Winnicott, 1971: 68). While Mrs Norton is not a psychotherapist, the extreme and negative versions of the children she held up to them in this lesson, and her use of them to display herself as clever, more knowing and sophisticated, has some resonances. The reaction is certainly likely to be similar: trauma and a reduction of creativity. What will it take for Muhi or Shanhrul to look in that mirror again? And what does it mean not to look? Unfortunately teachers often understand learners who do not turn to them to learn about themselves as arrogant. Is that how these boys might come to be understood?

An absent mirror

Relative to the white-heat of public exposure, the other extreme might be an experience of invisibility, of looking and finding no response. Sometimes teachers seemed more concerned about themselves and their own (non-teaching, adult-focussed) tasks than with the children. What impact does that have on learners? Lessons in which teachers were absorbed in their own, adult activities were infused with a sense of lostness:

> There is an atmosphere where the children 'get on with it' and the teachers do their best to ignore them. Miss Middleton is on the computer, planning again, and Mrs Norton is reading something. This lack of interest is reflected in the work ethic too, especially among the boys. Those at my table are discussing football, then they begin 'waxing' their arms with sticky labels. None of them seems overly concerned about finishing.
>
> (field notes)

If the mirror is absent, what can one learn, where should one turn? If learning could only be academic, if the geography or history could be separated from the person, perhaps this would not be an issue. But, as I have argued elsewhere (Bibby, 2009a), coming to know academic knowledge is intimately bound to the relationship in which it is learned. Academic- and self-knowledge are inseparable, not least because if I learn something new I have to adjust my sense of self from one-who-does-not-know to one-who-knows.

Being overlooked

More often, neither overt humiliation nor invisibility dominated; rather, classroom life was liberally peppered with small experiences of being looked over. In his book *Playing and Reality*, Winnicott (1971) reports his analysis with a patient who was concerned with 'establishing herself as an individual'. He reports her coming to a session and saying 'Wouldn't it be awful if the child looked into the mirror and saw nothing!' He goes on to explain that the rest of the material in the session 'concerned the environment provided by her mother when she was a baby, the picture being of a mother talking to someone else unless actively engaged in a positive relating to the baby. The implication here was that the baby would look at the mother and see her talking to someone else' (Winnicott, 1971: 156–57). This is redolent of the experience of the classroom: a place full of other people for the teacher to look at. On these occasions it is not so much that the mirror is completely absent, rather there are a number of small, temporary absences, moments when the teacher, scanning the room, can see others but not me. The experience of being overlooked, having someone chosen above oneself, is difficult, as Minnie explains:

Minnie: I always have my hand up and Miss South never picks me, like I had my hand up before Sally and Miss South picked Sally.
SC: That does sound difficult, how does it make you feel?
Minnie: Broken.

On a larger scale, during year 5 the boys (rightly) believed they were more likely to be seen for being naughty than helpful or hard-working, and some of the girls were expert at manipulating situations so that they would receive praise and the reward of small (domestic) jobs. The persistent inability to be seen in a positive light can, gradually, lead to disruptive and unhelpful behaviours. Over the course of year 5, Rhatul developed the (extremely annoying) habit of softly whistling under his breath on the carpet. He was a small child, often overlooked because there were a number of more demanding personalities in the class. Observing him over the course of several weeks, it became clear that the only way he felt able to receive attention was to become more demanding, and so he began to play up his scatty, noisy side and to soften this with impish smiles. The whistling had been barely noticeable until I saw a different teacher take the register and treat him positively; he was much more focussed, no whistling and generally more cooperative.

Conclusion

What are the mirrors that the classroom provides? How do children see themselves in these mirrors? What do they do with the images? And, why does this matter? Were the children involved with our project oversensitive? Were they making a fuss? Am I making a fuss? How can the judgements of others come to matter so much? Why do they impact our identities so strongly? Judith Butler has drawn attention to the power of a judgement:

> Called by an injurious name, I come into social being, and because I have a certain inevitable attachment to my existence, because a certain narcissism takes hold of any term that confers existence, I am led to embrace the terms that injure me because they constitute me socially . . . As a further paradox, then, only by occupying – being occupied by – that injurious term can I resist and oppose it, recasting the power that constitutes me as the power I oppose.
>
> (Butler, 1997: 104)

Butler is drawing attention to the link between symbolism (naming) and the mirror function of the Other. She is highlighting the psychic insistence that we pay attention to the labels, the 'injurious names', we are given. Even if we choose to reject these labels, we are responding to them and have therefore, paradoxically, accepted them.

While judgements and comments may be intended to be benign or helpful, we cannot be sure of their reception unless we engage with their receipt. And even then, we can never be absolutely sure. Communication is not the simple giving of a message, it is always incomplete, and there needs to be constant checking and construction of meaning. If this process is not engaged in then a kind of madness prevails in which I assume my words carry only one meaning (mine) and that their receipt has no implication beyond that meaning. Comments, judgements, are never neutral, they are always infused with extra meanings from the positions we occupy. The very gap between the object, the idea of the object and its symbolisation (its 'word'), between my understanding of an idea and yours, colours our meanings and communications, generating and compounding flows of affect. And, importantly, communication is a two-way process. While this chapter has focussed on the children's uses of the teacher's mirror-function, the service is mutual; teachers simultaneously receive messages about themselves from those they teach, and learners also look to each other.

The examples in this chapter come from the general day-to-day business of being in the classroom. Whatever the import or intent of comments and actions, all teacher communications are read assiduously by learners. It may be that age, institutional positioning and relative inexperience mean that young learners, in general, are more dependent on their teachers than teachers are on their learners. There is no simple answer here for teachers about how to behave or what to say. Any action, or non-action even, will be used as a mirror – we cannot preselect the images and messages that we hold up. This is part of the difficulty of living as social beings, part of the difficulty of teaching. Any of the comments we make, and the comments we fail to make, are available to be taken as an image of the self by any of the learners we work with. The question of how can the teacher act if this knowledge is accepted remains. Do we try to mirror constructively? Or should we help students recognise the fantasy that the judgement says something 'true' about them, and bring awareness of other judgements and realities that they might draw on? Since both of these are ideal positions and the desire to be able to do either one reliably is wishful thinking (a fantasy) perhaps the effort has to be to work with both, mindfully and collaboratively?

The Lacanian metaphor of the mirror gives us a tool with which to think through the implications of our communications. In wondering 'Who am I? What am I like?' and looking for an answer in 'How do you see me?', we come to misrecognise ourselves in the images provided by others. Our mistake, to go back to Dumbledore, is to believe that the mirror provides truth – although that is easier said than acted upon. As we notice the partial and distorted images of ourselves in the reactions of those around us (the mirrors), we pluck them like *coats from the bric-à-brac of a props department* and, whether we want to or not, we put them on. They become part of our sense of who we are. That is why they impact us so deeply. In putting on the layers of coats gifted through the judgements of others and identified in the Lacanian mirror, it helps if there is someone, a thoughtful Dumbledore, who can help us understand that we might be feeling strangled because we have put one on back-to-front.

4 Accountability

Winnicott in the playless classroom

This chapter builds on notions of mirroring and identification to consider the environment within which the mirroring takes place. I will draw on the work of the psychoanalyst Donald Winnicott to look at the context within which individual exchanges in classrooms occur. Winnicott's understanding of identification and ego formation is somewhat different from Lacan's but the divided, defended self and the dynamic unconscious remain at the heart of a Winnicottian version of the human condition. In particular, this chapter uses Winnicott's notion of the holding and handling environments, the maternal facilitating environment, to explore some effects of accountability on the learning environment.

The accountability culture that pervades the whole public sector has come to shape education at all levels. Schools are (perhaps understandably) obsessed with assessment as a technique for demonstrating their compliance with policy demands and as the means by which they can demonstrate that they are doing their jobs successfully. The potential costs of non-compliance are high: schools can lose their good name and receive labels that will scare away parents, children, and therefore money. In extreme cases schools can be closed down and reopened with new names and new senior management teams, destroying careers. Teachers' pay can suffer if they fail to reach threshold targets which are often phrased, in part at least, in terms of pupil performance. The move to a managerial ethic (Ball, 2003) has, it has been suggested, shifted attention from 'caring for' (children, each other) to 'caring about' (league tables, budgets, Office for Standards in Education, Children's Services and Skills (Ofsted)) (Forrester, 2005).

Within the classroom, the penetration of accountability demands is made most visible by the constant use of (formal and informal) tests; the culture of personal and permanent judgement that dominates the kinds of mirroring that children receive. Early in our research project, Mr Leader, the head teacher, explained his belief that SATs, the formal assessments required in primary school, were, in his school at least, containable and contained:

> SATs isn't a driver for the way we teach. It is not, I would say. Apart from three weeks before they take the test in year 6.

Despite his protestations, the single topic that came up most frequently (in interviews and observations) over the course of the research was tests: 'levels', how to do better at them, how you *should* be doing in them, how you actually *are* doing in them, how your peers are doing, and so on. A focus on measured attainment dominated the lessons: it structured teaching groups and filled teacher-talk and, to a lesser extent, children's conversations in interviews. Often, adults' language about tests and levels was aimed at the class in general rather than at individuals. What is the experience of being an individual in such a context? What kind of a mirror do assessments hold up? In what ways were the teachers able to 'be there', to feed, and enable, playful and creative responses to ideas? Is it true, as Gargiulo hints, that fragmentation and codification, such as we find in the National Curriculum, 'reduce spontaneity to reflex, creativity to formula and culture to control' (Gargiulo, 1998: 144)?

The previous chapter used Lacan's mirror stage to explore what mirroring in the classroom might look like, how it might be experienced and influence our sense of self. The metaphor of the mirror provided one way of thinking about processes of identification and misrecognition that are part of unconscious communication. The absolute difficulty of relating and communicating was indicated. Most notably we saw that the mirrors that were held up to children showed small, often distorted fragments of images. Without help in interpreting what they were 'seeing' of themselves, children were left to make what sense they could. Increasingly, these identifications were with numbers they felt little connection to and had less understanding of. A micro-focus on the ways in which comments, actions and judgements impact on our sense of self raises a question about the 'atmosphere' or ethos of a classroom. What happens if we lift our heads to look at the context in which teacher comments are made, the environment into which they are dropped and from which they are taken up?

Donald Winnicott, a facilitating environment, play and creativity

Winnicott is perhaps best known for his work on babies in relation to their first significant relationships (Winnicott, 1964). Given his interests in the very earliest stages of development, teachers in schools are presented with a difficulty in reading much of his work. If he spends so much time talking about newly nursing mothers (the mother–child dyad) and the experience of 'good-enough' (rather than 'ideal' or perfect) early mothering, what has that got to do with us? If he is talking about the nursery school, what has that got to do with secondary school? Or higher education?

It is important, though, to remember that his work can be read both literally and metaphorically. When we enter a new context, a new set of relationships, we are put back into positions of dependence. Clearly we are differently dependent than a newborn infant, but we *are* dependent. As we grow up, the visceral difficulties of dependency stay with us. Growing up means adding something, not losing the original states, and our responses to new situations are shaped by our earliest experiences. Induction programmes and the provision of personal tutors and mentors, for example, offer institutional recognition of a return to dependency when we are 'born' into a new context.

A significant criticism of psychoanalysis, and especially developmental accounts, is that they tend to idealise motherhood and then blame the mother for any difficulties that emerge later. Western culture celebrates the impossible fantasy of a 'dreaming, associative mother' utterly bound up with her new baby: completely absorbed by the child, and imbued not only with a telepathic ability to know what it wants, but also endless time and space to pay attention exclusively to its needs. However, Winnicott was a realist. There is never an idyll; for him the mother has only to be 'good-enough' for enough of the time. Indeed, following Klein, failure is seen as inevitable, and the frustrations and anger that failures engender are, he suggests, what motivate thought and development (this is explored further in chapters 7 and 8). Creating and blaming 'bad mothers', putting the 'bad' outside ourselves, is a form of defensive splitting. This raises questions about the anxieties that our (schools', society's) responsibilities to provide *good-enough* holding and handling environments (mothering) engender; what might it mean to deny our complicity, and to 'blame' [m]others?

For Winnicott, a good-enough facilitating environment enables the development of a 'true' or 'authentic' self-structure, while a sustained failure of the environment can lead to the defensive development of a 'false' or 'caretaker' self-structure. These are unfortunate labels but the sense of them will be explored later. He presents a complex developmental story. However, while the original maternal environment is important in that it creates a template for future relationships, it is also important to recognise that later relationships may challenge the template. Such challenges may be towards greater trust and integration – an aim of much psychoanalysis – or they may act more negatively, disrupting experiences of self-integrity without supporting reintegration. What, then, of the environment generated and sustained by a culture of accountability in a school?

A facilitating environment and a 'true' self-structure

There are three aspects of the mother–child relationship that, Winnicott suggests, facilitate development. First, the mother has to be a reliable presence; merely *being there* meets an emotional need. Second, the mother is needed to present the world to the baby. Winnicott describes how, by sensitively feeding the baby, by the mother allowing the breast to be present and not present appropriately, the child can develop a sense of itself as living in a space in which what it needs and desires are available. In this way she or he develops a sense of agency, although, since this is based in omnipotent fantasies (that the breast arrives *because* it is needed), it is illusory. Finally, the mother is needed to disillusion the baby, to enable the infant to move beyond omnipotent fantasies. This wider aspect of weaning refers to weaning the child off his own omnipotence and absolute dependence. In this movement, the child has to learn to tolerate frustration; needs will be met, but probably not the instant they are experienced.

Discussing Winnicott, Fonagy and Target explain that 'the true self can only evolve in the presence of an unobtrusive other who will not interrupt the continuity of experience of oneself' (2003: 142). Experiencing such continuity is dependent on three, inter-connected factors which are given as aspects of a *successful facilitating environment*: a sense of inner safety, 'an ability to limit concern with external events, and the generation of spontaneous, creative gestures' (Fonagy and Target, 2003: 142). Through the mother's good-enough mirroring and the child seeing itself and its internal states reasonably well reflected, it comes to experience itself as an integrated whole (rather than fragmented parts). A 'good-enough' relationship can bear the strains of aggression, anger, frustration and hate as well as the satisfactions of love and gratitude. In moving on from a state of phantasised omnipotence in which self and mother were one, the child is enabled to bear the ambivalence it feels towards the real-mother who exists 'out there' (simultaneously loved and hated), its guilt at the aggression it meted out (in phantasy and in biting, pulling, hitting), and its anxiety lest she seek revenge. These dimensions and actions are a necessary part of all relations with a parental dimension, including later pedagogic relations.

A sense of inner safety can develop if needs and desires are acknowledged and managed or satisfied appropriately. In school, this might take place if 'feeding' is sensitively managed and a child's interests are recognised and given some space. The image of the baby at its mother's breast can be hard to move beyond but education is replete with feeding metaphors and the nourishment that a good learning experience can provide. The metaphors that connect teaching and learning to food and feeding cover the full range of things that people do with food – from *cooking up a plan*, through *taking in, absorbing* and *digesting* knowledge, to having *thoughts that make us sick* and *ideas that are shit*. We go on *taster courses* and *get the flavour of a book*. Thoughts and actions can be *unsavoury, tasteless* or otherwise *unpalatable*, or they may be *spicy* and *get our juices flowing*. We sometimes admit that students are required to *regurgitate information* in a test or examination. We can have *thirst for knowledge* or *be hungry for new experiences* perhaps because we feel *empty headed*. We might *chew over* new ideas or leave them to *simmer on the back-burner* but recoil when someone *spits* words or ideas at us, and are left feeling uncomfortable if something is *too much to take in* perhaps because we have *bitten off more than we can chew*.

If education is about taking in and digesting ideas and information, what does it mean for schooling and lessons to be compulsory? And what does it signify for there to be places and topics to which we cannot say no? There would seem to be some implication that the 'food' (ideas, topics, subjects, ways of thinking) offered by the school and teacher will be universally experienced as desirable and pleasurable (no overcooked sprouts here), that students will always be hungry and therefore ready for new things to ingest. Which ideas are the mental equivalents of a packet of chocolate biscuits? And, however much one likes chocolate biscuits, are they always what we want? Who are the educational compulsive eaters? Where in the education system can we recognise learners who might have unhealthy relationships with the food (ideas, knowledge) and feeding (teaching, learning)? Can we even imagine such people?

In a consideration of the minutiae of feeding, Winnicott talks at length about the way a baby will take what it wants at a rate it finds pleasure (excitement) in. Acts of turning away and back are, he suggests, part of a self-regulation of the pleasure, of enjoying the moment. But he recognises that mothers who 'long to get on with being generous' (Winnicott, 1964: 48) sometimes cannot bear the tension (physically or emotionally) of slow feeding and can want to rush a child into feeding at her pace. But he cautions against haste or forcing; the development of trust through patience, sensitivity, and being able to bracket off one's own concerns and hold these separate, will lead to a better experience. Later in his book *The Child, the Family and the Outside World*, he picks this up and contemplates the move from the mother to the teacher:

> Feeding is never simply a matter of getting food in; it is another way in which the school teacher continues the work of the mother. The school, like the mother, shows love by feeding the child, and, like the mother, expects to be refused (hated, suspected) as well as accepted (trusted). In the nursery school there is no place for what is impersonal or mechanical, because, for the child, this means hostility or (worse still) indifference.
>
> (Winnicott, 1964: 194)

He suggests,

> Good teaching demands of the teacher a toleration of the frustrations to his or her spontaneity of giving, or feeding – frustrations that may be felt acutely. The child, in learning to be civilised, naturally also feels frustrations acutely, and is helped in becoming civilised not so much by the teacher's precepts as by the teacher's own ability to bear the frustrations inherent in teaching.
>
> (Winnicott, 1964: 202–3)

This is easier said than done. I wonder whether, in conditions where accountability is king, the school or a teacher can still tolerate a refusal of knowledge, or whether the pressure to be feeding at all times has come to override other sensibilities? Is a rejection too dangerous to bear if you are being judged by how wonderfully fat your baby is growing?

Time is always revealed as a preoccupation in interviews with teachers – there is never enough of it and the demands made on what there is can feel unbearable (see for example Acker, 1999). The interviews we conducted with teachers generally indicated the pressure they felt under to 'shove', 'hammer', 'push', 'cram' and 'force' knowledge into children so that they would make at least the expected progress. Only one teacher, Lisa Warner, said anything that suggested this force-feeding might be counterproductive, and even then, until the exams were over, she felt she had to keep going:

> My year [year 6] is very heavy on testing . . . And I think I am quite didactic in that I have always got a good idea about what I want the children to do, and the end product. And I know I am quite fixed like that. And I know that in some subjects, and for some children, I ought to lighten up a bit. What I tend to do is show good examples of work from previous years, and in a way what I am saying is I am expecting all of you to [produce work like this] but actually what I probably should be doing is not showing them the good examples and letting them be a bit more free about what they do . . . I will when the exams are over . . . I thought I would try and . . . reduce the amount that I am talking and try to improve the amount of practical, open-ended tasks I give the children to do . . . I've got this idea of myself as being entertaining and being good at teaching things and good at explaining things. But I also know that however good I am, it really doesn't matter if the children aren't learning. So I might think I am bloody entertaining out there, but it doesn't matter diddly squat does it, if the children aren't learning? So if they can learn better because I shut up, and let them struggle a bit more, I think that is what I need to do. I think I reduce the struggle too much.

The pull Lisa is experiencing between the demands from outside the classroom and the children's needs inside the classroom is palpable. And in this tug-of-war, the outside is winning. Once the exams are over, the tension will abate and she anticipates that she will be able to attend to the children's needs. To manage the pressure at the moment she spoon-feeds them, breaking up the knowledge into easily swallowed lumps so they will not need to struggle to get it down. The way Lisa manages external events and her own tensions passes the pressure she experiences to the children; from their perspective she may seem to be failing to manage those external events at all.

This management of external events is important and, in an assessment culture, the need to protect vulnerable others from (some) outside demands might easily be overlooked. Indeed, the demand may be experienced as unbearable; facing our own responsibility and grown-up-ness can be terrifying, for where does it leave our fragile vulnerabilities? Who is going to protect us? Such unbearable tensions can result in defensive splitting. In such a move, our bad and uncaring sides can be disavowed and experienced as belonging to 'bad mothers', 'bad teachers', 'bad politicians', 'bad anyone-but-me'. Simultaneously, our unbearable vulnerability can be projected on to the learners, leaving us apparently strong enough to cope but cut off from the experience of vulnerability that would enable us to act empathically.

A culture of accountability encourages bureaucratic, jobs-worth responses, perhaps particularly to demands that we stand up and shelter more vulnerable others. While Mr Leader can say that SATs are not drivers in his school, if he monitors teachers' and children's progress in terms of National Curriculum levels, we might suggest that he is insisting that those more vulnerable than himself (the teachers in his school) are being forced to attend to external factors that they do not have the resources to manage, and so stress cascades down to those least able to stand up for themselves. The tension belongs higher up the food chain, ultimately with the politicians whose desire to be seen to be making a difference and for re-election turns education into a political football. The failure to manage the tension ends up with those least able to protect themselves; failures occur repeatedly at all points north. Accountability seems to have become a defensive response to the unknown demands of the other.

'Feeding' in the classroom is generally done at the teachers' pace with little time to draw breath, chew or digest ideas; this pace, like expectations for progress, can be relentless. To facilitate feeding in Grafton School, the children were grouped according to some notion of ability. This practice, once restricted to secondary schools, has found its way into primary schools, and is particularly used in the teaching of the 'core' subjects, mathematics and English. At Grafton School teachers 'split' the two parallel classes into three for these subjects. This splitting was done on the basis of 'ability' and National Curriculum levels were taken as a proxy measure of this ability. In this way assessment, and tests that measured assessment, shaped the classroom environment, particularly the mathematics and English groups. Ability groupings are institutional defences that manage teacher anxieties about 'appropriate feeding', but they create anxieties for those within them.

The children were aware of what group they were in and what this meant, although they tended to use more straightforward, less euphemistic terminology than the teachers. So they referred to the 'clever', 'cleverest' and 'bottom' groups. Some of the children talked about how much stress was associated with being in a top or middle group since the prospect of 'moving down' always loomed, generating a climate of fear. The children who had been moved up or down were talked about like spectres whose missing presence was a reminder of the need to constantly 'work hard':

> The children tell me they've been put in levels 'and we're the cleverest'. Shamima reports ominously that three children have been kicked out of this group because 'they weren't working as hard as they used to'. Almost as if she is considering her own fate, she then quickly returns to her work.
>
> (field notes)

Meanwhile, children who had been 'moved down' struggled to make sense of their demotion. Many of the children in the lowest maths group were happy to be there and liked the fact that their teacher, Miss Middleton, did not challenge them and so provided a safe, if not very mathematical, environment. But for Muhi, who had recently been demoted from the middle group, the experience was more problematic. Indeed, he seemed unable to recognise himself in this environment; a great sadness would be if he decided he could:

Muhi: Yeah, I got to the lowest [group]. And Miss Middleton hates maths, so guess what she does? She says 'right, get all your times tables done' and then she gets paper and we just have to colour, like reception.
Matthew: Miss Middleton is fun. I wish I was in her maths group.
Muhi: But she hates maths. She doesn't even learn us maths. It's [very] boring, we just had to colour like reception [. . .]
Emran: When Miss Middleton took us just for a bit she never taught us it and I think it was just a waste, I don't know, of teaching. Because I learned more from when we had to do sticking to make a collage.

In this extract, Matthew, who used to work with Muhi in the middle group, seems to try to make it okay for him to be in Miss Middleton's bottom maths group; it must be fun. But for Muhi there was only frustration; he was left not learning a subject he used to enjoy and he felt diminished by the experience. Eventually Emran confirmed his interpretation of the lessons: little learning happened. We need to ask: What does Muhi see when he looks for himself in this non-maths mathematics group? Muhi-who-likes-maths has become invisible to himself, he is alienated from his previous self. He will have to re-write that part of his identity so that he can 'see' himself in his new location, and that rewrite will come at a heavy cost to his mathematics learning identity.

Given that 'levels' shaped their classroom environment so strongly, it was disturbing to note that the children had little understanding of what they were, beyond a number. Indeed, whether the numbers indicated a place or a rate of progress was sometimes unclear. In the spring term of year 5 (more than a year before the SATs), Miss South explained to the children that they all had to 'hit targets' for their learning. She asked what they thought their targets were but the children's apparently random suggestions were eventually ignored. She went on to explain that their target was to 'move up two sub-levels a year' and that, as they were currently about half-way through the year, that meant they should have already moved up one sub-level. There was no explanation about what a level or a sub-level was, but she went on to tell them that she knew they were making good progress. There was going to be a meeting soon with Mr Leader to tell him how well they were doing. 'So,' she warned them, 'you can't sit back. You need to work really, really hard to the end of the year to make sure you've all gone up two or even more.' Her slippage from the individual to the collective makes it unclear whose responsibility progress is: the children's or hers.

Although there was uncertainty about expectations for progress through the levels, doing well and being well regarded were understood to be very important:

TB: What does it mean to be a level 5?

Sally: I don't know. It's just more or less the teachers are always proud of you and then they mention your name in class. [When they say my name] I feel very proud of myself [. . .] Like, last year when I got a level 5 I was like the top of my group and then Miss South she always said my name during lessons . . . I liked that.

Unfortunately for the majority of the class, only one person at a time can come top. What sense, therefore, did children make of these levels and the expectation that they would make relentless progress? In no conversation was a child able to tell us what a level meant except in terms of whether it was good enough (it never was). They were not able to express what they needed to do to improve their level except in general terms, and these tended to feel impossible:

AH: Do you know what you need to do to get to level 4?

Minnie: No idea.

Yasmin: Concentrate, focus, listen to all the teacher's lessons, which I can't do.

The general notion of levels gives us a sense of the extent to which tests and the results of testing permeated and infused the classroom structures. However, this environment was neither monolithic nor static, it was constructed by the teachers in response to curriculum subjects, particular topics, their own sense of professionalism, the wider culture of teaching and so on. Thinking back to the suggestion that, to develop a 'true' self-structure, children need an *unobtrusive other who will not interrupt the continuity of experience of oneself*, it seems clear that, for some at least, this is not what was happening. In the name of the ability groups, and for the best of reasons (children were reshuffled into other groups so they got the 'right' teaching), children were being denied continuity of self-experience. The classroom was a place of impossible demand – for even, linear progress – and this external demand for perfection caught the children in 'a hall of mirrors' (Gargiulo, 1998: 151).

Finally, Winnicott's suggestion is that a facilitating environment supports attempts to respond creatively to life, to play, and, ultimately, provides access to culture, to shared expressions of life experiences. For Winnicott, creativity does not relate only to the production of art or music, it is any response to internal states: a cry, a movement, a word.[1] We can see how, as we mature and the range of responses available to us increases, 'creative gestures' might turn into music, literature, mathematics, and so forth, but to limit our understanding of creativity to such mature, codified responses is to do ourselves an injustice. Similarly, central to

Winnicott is his understanding that play is not a mindless, recreational activity. His use of the concept of 'transitional objects' that can mediate between 'me' and 'not me' extends beyond the blanket and teddy bear to culture: 'In the creation of culture man weaves the not me with his subjective phantasies and produces a world in which he feels safe enough to play' (Gargiulo, 1998: 144). Play involves creativity rather than rule-following, there is a degree of spontaneity and involvement or concentration, a wrapped-up-in-it-ness that speaks of engagement and focus. To emphasise: Winnicott's position is that creativity and play are movements that emerge from a subjective experience, from *our* desire to express something of our internal states, *not* as a response to the imagined desire of the Other. In a world dominated by accountability, and therefore full of the expectations of others, this might be more difficult to understand and act on than we might like to think.

Philip Pullman, the children's author, has been highly critical of the teaching of literacy in schools. His explanation of the writing process links strongly to a Winnicottian notion of creativity:

> I'm thinking of the teacher who asked for my advice for her pupils who would shortly be confronted with a SAT, where the rubric for the writing test told them to spend exactly 15 minutes on planning their story, and 45 minutes on writing it. Proper writing just doesn't happen like that.
>
> Nor does it always go through the process of planning, drafting, re-drafting, polishing and editing, which teachers are also required to put their unfortunate pupils through. Nor does every piece of work have to be completed. Some stories you aren't ready to write yet, so you put them away for six months or two years and come back to them when you're ready.
>
> There are no rules. Anything that's any good has to be discovered in the process of writing it. Furthermore, there must be a willing suspension of certainty . . . We cannot require everything to take place under the bright glare of discussion and checking and testing and consultation: some things require to be private and tentative.
>
> (Pullman, 2003: 6)

In the context of writing, why does anyone write? What is the purpose of writing? A novel generally aims to entertain and to move its reader. To respond to a request for a story or a picture requires some contact with our own experiences so that we can have something to say, something to convey. Writing non-fiction and working on mathematics are no less subjective; conveying interest and knowledge also requires contact with our inner-lives. Focussing on technical aspects ahead of knowing what we want to say severs our connection to our subjectivities and results in a fracturing, another loss of a sense of continuity of self. Like Winnicott's overanxious mother forcing the child to attend to the breast when it is trying to savour some other moment, if the demand of the Other (the teacher, the audience, the test-marker) insists on primacy it forces attention outside the self and away from the creative gesture.

A failed facilitating environment and a 'caretaker' self-structure

A failure in the facilitating environment may come about if the child's needs or states cannot be 'seen' and well enough 'mirrored' by the mother, or if the presentation of the world (the 'feeding') lacks sensitivity. Fonagy and Target explain that, while a child may be taught to say 'thanks' on receipt of something, the word is uttered because it has been demanded, not as a creative response to an internal experience of gratitude.

Psychoanalytically, if the mother's 'mirroring' bears no relation to the experiences of the child then symbolic communication will not develop. Chapter 3 explored such difficulties in the classroom. Each mis-mirroring and mis-giving amounts to an 'impingement' on the child's experience of itself; a violence that, if repeated often enough, may become traumatic:

> According to Winnicott when impingements continue despite persistence by the infant, a number of reactions can arise: the self may be overwhelmed, it may anxiously anticipate further impingement, it may feel real only in opposition to impingements, or finally it can acquiesce and hide its own gestures. In this latter case, Winnicott assumed that the self ends up mimicking its caretaking environment, resigned to the deficiency, setting aside creative gestures and perhaps forgetting they ever existed. Winnicott suggested that the infant compliantly relates to the caretaker's gestures as if they were his own, and this lies at the root of the *false self-structure*. The false self is marked by a lack of spontaneity or originality.
>
> (Fonagy and Target, 2003: 143)

So, if the facilitating environment fails, we are faced with a very different set of conditions. An ability to play creatively is transformed into compliance as the sense of connection to the inner world becomes fractured. If my creative gestures, suggestions and ideas are repeatedly rejected, I will experience no need to look inwards for inspiration. Marcus and Rosenberg explain that, for Winnicott, 'without a "facilitating environment" the child was likely to develop a false self . . . in part characterised by compulsively anticipating the reactions of others' (1998: 141). If a child (teacher or anyone else) has no reason to look to their own subjective responses for learning, then, realising that the demands of the other are where rewards lie, they learn to anticipate those demands and become compliant. Or, if they refuse the demands and respond to their own subjective responses, they become 'non-compliant'.

Unfortunately, classrooms are full of examples of teachers, either deliberately or accidentally, consciously or unconsciously, ignoring or rejecting children's ideas. Whatever the teachers' intentions, these are often felt to be deliberate by the children who suffer endless small hurts. In Grafton School, mathematics lessons were full of ignored responses. Often having a response ignored is interpreted as 'that is the wrong answer', and sometimes it is, but not always. With the teachers narrowly focussed on the technical aspects of writing, especially what they called 'vcop' (vocabulary, connectives, openers and punctuation), any notion that writing is a subjective business was systematically excised. In this way the children stopped trying to write stories that came from a connection with their lives and instead sought to perform 'interesting words', even if these were not appropriate.

For children whose vocabulary comes largely from school activities and reading, a limited understanding of words can become even more problematic and there are many comments in our field notes about children stopping asking what words mean and instead asking whether they are interesting. Lists of 'connectives' associated with levels were stuck onto the fronts of children's books and, although these were meant only as examples, they became the connectives of choice. Strange confections developed although the children were repeatedly reminded, 'If you keep using "and" what level will you stay at? One.' Clearly not an acceptable option! The following long extract describes a typical year 6 English lesson in which Mrs Norton drew on assessment for learning practices.

They have written out little 'stories' in their books and now they are going to evaluate them on their own. First they are meant to underline all the connectives they've used. I find myself unclear on what a connective is and Sally is disappointed when I tell her I don't know. 'Well you're no help,' she says, flipping back through her book to find them. Mrs Norton asks them to look at their work and if the only connectives they've used have been 'and' or simple connectives then they're only at level one. Sally puts up her hand to report that she has used 'however' and the teacher tells her, 'Good.' Sally complains to me that when Mrs Norton marks her book 'there's always something wrong, I always have to improve.' . . .

The next task is to look through and find any 'interesting openings'. Katie is scanning her piece and she reads out 'When the three weird sisters . . .' then raises her eyebrow and asks me 'Interesting?' This makes me laugh but I also think it's emblematic of the increased self-regulation the children are being asked to undertake . . . Next they move on to punctuation and Mrs Norton points out the 'punctuation pyramid' which is hanging in their classroom. She wants to know how many of them used a bracket, a dash or an ellipsis in their sentence. Sally points out that she has used brackets but very few others have used similar (level five) punctuation. 'Now you can see that we have to up that level' Mrs N tells them. At the end of the lesson they are asked, 'If you had to write a comment on your writing, what would it be?' She gives an example of 'I need to remember to write . . .' or 'I could improve on –'. So apparently you can't say how brilliant your piece was. In fact there is no choice over whether you wish to write this or not and Sally dutifully adds 'I need to use my VCOP to improve my writing.'

(field notes)

The slow death of enjoyment was accompanied by the children finding other sources of pleasure. The conjoined need to conform and perform encouraged competitive pleasures, typically the completion of lines in English or racing down pages of questions in mathematics. In these races, accuracy was rejected and a strange blindness developed. For example, an exercise in the mathematics scheme had paired calculations written out thus:

1) 42×21 42×19
2) 24×21 24×19
3) 16×21 16×19

The intention here was clearly to work the paired calculations together using a significantly simpler calculation ($\times 20$ and $\pm \times 1$). However, the boys I was sitting with asked the teacher whether they had to work across or down one column and then the other. She had not spotted the link and so told them to work down the page and they did not feel able to look and think about what would be best. A learning opportunity that had been constructed by the scheme writers was lost but an opportunity to race down columns had been gained – much more satisfying in a classroom where creative thought was not valued. Ultimately, this 'stripped down' motivation was fuelled by an overwhelming and terrifying anxiety rather than the tolerable anxiety that facilitates curiosity.

A significant aspect of the classroom environment was the lack of playfulness. This ranged from the teachers' planning which was shared and often taken from the Internet or published schemes of work, through the uses of literature and dramatic expression, to children's responses to demands for their own creativity. It was notable, for example, that when children were to put on a play at Christmas or in celebration of the end of the school year, scripted versions were bought and the children were 'plugged into' the ready-made parts. Moments when schemes planned in opportunities for creativity or playfulness were often missed or passed over. During year 5, the children studied an abridged version of Shakespeare's *The Tempest*; simultaneously they were working on newspapers and had to consider the 'elements' of a front page. Rather than seeking out or creating a front-page relating to a shipwreck (such as the one that provides the backdrop to *The Tempest*), a potentially newsworthy event, or looking at a selection of the day's newspapers, the class studied an inauthentic 'Front Page' that the scheme had provided. Faced with apparent opportunities to respond creatively to stimuli, children reacted with disbelief and sought what they assumed was wanted.

The distinction between a 'true' and a 'false' or 'caretaker self' makes use of unfortunate labels but relates to some notion of authenticity, the extent to which any one of us is able to tolerate our vulnerability. To be able to accept and regulate anxiety about constitutive vulnerability requires some ability to trust self and others, a trust that, as Winnicott suggests, develops in a good-enough facilitating environment. Children's work is like an offering, a gift to their teacher, and the way that the teacher responds to that is very important to the child. While a teacher's focus may be on the content of the gift, the child's focus is on the overall receipt of the gift. Sally and Minnie explained this in an interview, in which they were commenting on the actions of their new year 6 teacher, Miss Warner:

Sally: . . . when she saw us she said she heard we were a really good class but I don't know if she believes that. But we had to make little books introducing ourselves. What she did was she just put them in this box, like a scrap box, and I'm sure I saw Fatima's ripped and Muhi's ripped so she doesn't exactly take care.

Minnie: I think on the outside she likes us and she's just saying, I think she's lying, but inside I think she's saying, 'I don't like this classroom'.

Sally and Minnie seem to fear that the lack of care taken to protect the work is a predictor of a lack of effort to take care of them. Their work appears to stand as a proxy for themselves, a significance Miss Warner seems unaware of. Perhaps that is why, given a mark and some formative comments, the teacher will focus on the formative comments but, until trust is established, the learner will focus on the mark (Butler, 1988).

Conclusion

By failing to stand between the learner and the demands of the institution (in the case of a school: Ofsted, the government, school and local authority targets), the teacher fails to protect the child (and herself) from hostile elements in the environment. These distract her and, in her distraction and her self-protectiveness, she may fail to provide 'good-enough' experiences of mirroring, feeding and careful 'weaning' so that the child has to take care of itself. And when an individual has to provide their own protection in a situation where they could reasonably have expected help: 'Self awareness can be, all too easily, a by-product of the anxious ego, a hindrance to inventiveness . . . That individual becomes . . . both caretaker and cared for, overly self-conscious and apprehensively cautious; the caretaker-self is caught in a hall of mirrors' (Gargiulo, 1998: 150–51). Ironically, of course, in their own ways, local authorities fail to provide 'good-enough' environments for school managers, and school managements fail their teachers: the deprivation cascades down.

Earlier, I suggested that a 'good-enough' relationship can bear the strains of aggression, anger, frustration and hate as well as the satisfactions of love and gratitude. There was no evidence of any teacher awareness of the aggression that was undoubtedly in the room. While the occasional eruptions amongst the children were dealt with from time to time, and the room appeared generally orderly, the children carried frustrations and disappointments about their own sense of invisibility or not being worthy of love and attention. They hid their angry disappointment well, but it emerged in interviews directly ('If I were Miss South, yeah, and Miss South were me, I'd squash her like a fly') or indirectly, especially in frequent claims of 'unfairness'.

Rejecting or reacting angrily to the parental figure of the teacher was known to be unsafe. Teachers moved children in and out of groups, from one table to another, separating friends, and reducing opportunities for collaboration. In ending warm connections and isolating individuals the teachers caused small social 'deaths'; this was a hostile and frightening dimension of classroom life. There was no dialogue between children and teachers (or, as far as we saw, between teachers either) about the experience of the classroom or lessons, no sense of what the children might want to study; even good ideas were passed over if they did not fit the narrow remit in the teacher's head at that moment.

In all the lessons we observed there was never one that deviated onto a path that sprang from a child's idea. Teachers made it clear in formal and informal interviews that such a course of action was impossible; the teachers' plans were the only plans. Winnicott warned against this kind of intellectual domination. For him, the good-enough classroom would need to provide opportunities for playfulness, and give and take would require 'mutual sacrifice of spontaneity and independence'. While what a child wants to do cannot dominate *all* of the time, for it *never* to find expression would be deplorable. The creativity of both children and teachers requires recognition and some hope of bearing fruit. As Winnicott warned:

> At any rate, education is poor stuff, even when the subjects are well taught, if this object lesson – 'give and take' – is absent, or is overridden by dominance of one personality over another.
>
> [. . .] nothing is more misleading in the assessment of educational methods than simple academic success or failure. Success may so easily mean no more than that a child has found that the easiest way to deal with a particular teacher, or a particular subject, or with education as a whole, is by subservience, a holding open of the mouth with the eyes shut, or swallowing whole without critical inspection.
>
> (1964: 203)

5   Tall poppies and shrinking violets

Freud, Foulkes and the nature of groups

This chapter explores what groups are, how they are held together and maintained. Given education's, the school's and teachers' valorisation of the individual, the focus here is on the work children do in groups as well as on the consequences of that work. Faced with the demand to achieve the highest possible standings in the local league tables, and the highest possible National Curriculum levels for children, the mass of children together can come to be seen as a pragmatic convenience but an organisational nightmare: they squabble, argue, gossip, insist on playing in work time and resist learning. Why would a teacher not feel overwhelmed when there are 30 of *them* and only one of her? Here we look at what lies behind some of these non-compliant and annoying (to adults) behaviours as they relate to the formation and maintenance of groups. Groups are fundamental to the way we live and organise our lives, they permeate our ways of being and thinking but the chapters so far have focussed on individuals. The culture within education at the time of writing is very much of individuality, and personalised learning has come to dominate the framing of many social and educational policies. As Stephen Ball notes:

> The *personalisation* process is a relatively new one on the educational policy agenda . . . The extent to which the rhetoric of personalisation is translated into institutional and classroom practices remains to be seen but it will provide new opportunities for forms of differentiation and social advantage-seeking that interested parents will undoubtedly pursue . . . [P]ersonalisation is one instance of an emphasis within social and educational policy on individualism, the making of the individual within and the subject of policy . . . Individuals are required 'to make something of their lives and use their ability and potential to the full' (Blair, 2002). All of this encourages individualistic engagements with and responses to policy.
>
> (Ball, 2008: 204, emphasis in the original)

Does education need to be an individual endeavour? Is it possible to sustain the idea of group examinations? What might it mean for GCSEs or degrees to be awarded to individuals on the basis of group work? Valuing the larger group, and allowing ourselves not to matter so much for a moment, can be hard to sustain. Western tradition privileges the individual over the social; it is Descartes' legacy that we think of ourselves as residing in our heads, our selves bounded by our skin. We may acknowledge that we are also part of groups but at core many of us continue to believe there exists an essential *me* who is able to remain undissolved within, and continues to exist beyond, those groups. Psychoanalysis, however, offers an important challenge to the primacy of the individual, with Freud himself recognising our group nature:

> [O]nly rarely and under certain exceptional circumstances is individual psychology in a position to disregard the relations of this individual to others. In the individual's mental life someone else is invariably involved, as a model, as an object, as a helper, as an opponent; and so from the very first individual psychology, in this extended but entirely justifiable sense of the words, is at the same time social psychology as well.
>
> (Freud, 1921: 69)

Freud recognised people as developing out of their identifications and interactions within groups. Later, group psychoanalytic theorists such as Wilfred Bion and S. H. Foulkes[1] explored and developed his ideas. Foulkes' understanding of humanity as 'social through and through' (Pines, 1994: 48) offers a radical challenge to our thinking:

> Human beings always live in groups. Groups in turn cannot be understood, except in their relation to other groups and in the context of the conditions in which they exist . . . [T]he distinction between group and individual psychodynamics is meaningless, except . . . by abstraction. We sometimes talk of group and individual separately, as we focus more on one or other aspect of what is in fact one single and inseparable process.
>
> (Foulkes, 1966: 151–52)

An important conceptual shift made by Bion and Foulkes was to see the group itself as a unit of analysis. This directs attention away from the intrapsychic demands of the individual and towards the sheer, persistent difficulty of being and working in a group (the interpersonal playing out of the difficulties of living with one's internal, hidden groups) and the often apparently perverse difficulty we have in learning from experience.

This chapter and the next therefore explore aspects of education's failure to recognise and engage with this mutual implication of group and individual processes. In different ways, they ask what it might mean for young children to have their involvement in and explorations of groups and relatedness dismissed by adults as 'fussing' or as belonging in the playground. What work do children undertake to understand and maintain their group or social selves? The chapter explores what a group is, our ambivalent relations to groups, and group processes.

Groups to learn in

All educational establishments put students into groups: form groups (also called classes), tutor groups, seminar groups, lecture groups, year groups, top (and bottom) sets and streams. Some of these groups are together for extended periods of time. Children in primary school, for example, can be in the same class for all or most of their lessons for six years; form groups in secondary schools will spend long periods together but may be reconstituted for subject choices or streaming or setting purposes. In other contexts, the groups may be less intimate and shorter-lived. First-year lectures at university can contain very many students and offer few opportunities for interaction while the smaller seminar groups may meet only for the duration of aspects of the course, perhaps over 10 weeks or a term.

In Grafton School, the teachers combined and reformulated groups particularly for the teaching of literacy and numeracy. The two class teachers and one support teacher assigned to each year group meant that each group could be smaller than the class as a whole. This frequent regrouping meant that the school day was characterised by a high degree of turbulence. It would be possible for a child to come into the classroom for registration with the class teacher, then go to a different room for literacy with another teacher, and yet a further room for numeracy with someone else, before going back into the class group in the afternoon for other subjects. The field notes frequently record the fragmentation and occasional sense of disorientation experienced by the researchers and commented on, from time to time, by the children.

Despite the organisational effort that is put into arranging and managing groups, most of the academic work within 'groups' is undertaken by individuals – the groupings are more collections of individuals than groups (Alexander, Rose and Woodhead, 1992). Even where group work is encouraged, it is rare for final outputs (projects, essays, examinations) to be anything other than individual creations. This focus on the individual rather than the group maintains the tension we experience between our desire to belong and our desire to stand out, to be the same *and* different. Group psychoanalytic theories enable us to look more closely at this tension and to consider what is being silenced, denied, lost in current practices; what is rendered invisible, impossible and so on.

What is a group?

Teachers group learners together for a variety of reasons although it may not always be clear whether a collection of individuals assembled by someone else actually constitutes a 'group'. What is a group? If I collect together a number of children because I think they share some attribute, does that make them a group?

And if not, what has to happen for them to come to recognise themselves as a group? (The vexed question of whether any collection of people *can* work as a group and what that might mean is explored in the next chapter.)

Drawing on earlier writers, Freud defines some key aspects of groups.[2] These are familiar but are worth listing and bearing in mind:

1   a group experiences some degree of continuity to its existence
2   members of a group have some notion about what the group is – its form and function
3   groups need to interact with other groups
4   groups have traditions, customs and habits especially those that give individuals a place within the group
5   groups have a definite structure.

(Freud, 1921: 86)

Freud asserted that for groups to be able to work as a unit, all five conditions needed to be met. In terms of schools and other learning institutions, continuity is provided by our habit of collecting cohorts together according to age or year of study, and of keeping these groups together, sometimes for years at a time (although some schools and classes exhibit considerable turbulence, the institution itself can also provide continuity). Learning institutions are also strong on rituals and patterns of behaviour – with timetabling and assessment regimes providing a high degree of certainty over much that happens on a daily, weekly, termly and annual basis. However, the second, third and fifth requirements might be more problematic. Groups gathered for a temporary purpose may not be clear about what their purpose is, especially if it is a matter of expediency for the teacher. Opportunities for interaction between groups can be severely curtailed when they are kept isolated. This can happen, for example, when children are gathered around tables for particular subjects but are given little or no chance to communicate across the tables. And the structure of teaching groups is often far from clear. If groups are arranged according to some notion of 'ability', then teachers may feel an ethical responsibility not to communicate the structuring (although children are generally very aware of it). Within the group all individuals are expected to act independently: a group of children seated together to write stories rarely write one story, the sharing of ideas may be frowned upon, there is no scribe, no one person responsible for feeding back to the class and so on.

It is notable that particular forms of words are often prescribed to give groups a sense of function and purpose: *we are gathered here today* . . . Children (and other learners) often are not clear about, and therefore generate narratives to explain, the purposes and structures of the groups they find themselves in. Groups in a learning setting are often fairly arbitrary; they may have been brought together by fate, geography or presumed shared interests; as such, the groups may be difficult to define. Groups, such as those formed around the tables children are seated at, can

seem to have no function other than (for example) 'to do geography'. Such a neb-
ulous function is open to wide interpretation; it is also amenable to rejection – in
which case the group may decide it has another function, perhaps to entertain
itself.

Learners also recognise the fault lines that fracture and divide the many sub-
groups that exist in every larger group. These fault lines are much researched. The
structures and cultural negotiations of groups based around (for example) femininities (Hey, 1997; Reay, 2001a), masculinities (Frosh, Phoenix and Pattman,
2002), ethnicity (Shain, 2003) and social class (Lucey, 2001; Reay, 2002) have provided us with many insights into the work that individuals and groups do to define
and defend themselves. Since we are never just one thing, the difficulties of operating in the overlaps and interstices between groups are also increasingly recognised, and studies of what has been termed 'intersectionality' explore the ways that
groups interact intra- and inter-personally to support and undermine ways of
being in the world (see for example, Walkerdine, Lucey and Melody, 2001).

In Grafton School, issues of class, 'race' and gender were all important although
the most common marker discussed with the researchers was 'cleverness' or 'ability', an attribute that was sought and explored with increasing urgency as the year
6 SATs approached.

AH: How is it decided who goes into which group?
Minnie: Miss South decides.
AH: Do you know why she chooses different people for different groups?
Minnie: Well, we're the clever ones and they're like the cleverest!

Of course, 'cleverness' or relative achievement is, like 'race', class and gender, not
in the official curriculum; rarely are these topics open for discussion in classrooms.
Or at least, they are rarely the topic of discussions sanctioned by adult attention.
All children are able to inform visitors what it means to be in red rather than blue
group, or in Miss Jones' rather than Miss Smith's maths group. They know that it
matters how they are judged and that such judgements bring differential treatment
and opportunities. That the teachers we observed seemed unwilling or unable to
engage in these discussions, or to be open about their reasons for putting pupils in
groups, fooled no one. It is worth exploring more carefully what is at stake in *not*
discussing issues of group functions.

Even religion, which was on the curriculum, was not widely discussed in
Grafton School. Or rather, there were Religious Education lessons in which
aspects of religious observance or sacred texts were taught (we witnessed the
teaching of Sikhism and Buddhism in a school where most of the children were
from either Christian or Muslim traditions). But what it meant to be a Muslim in a
'broadly Christian' country during the second Iraq war, during the times of the
toppling and hanging of Saddam Hussein, following the 7 July bombings and so
on was not discussed, nor were the local tensions between Somali and Bangladeshi

Muslims on the adult/child agenda although children worried about and commented on these issues amongst themselves. In these small ways the children were held outside society, perhaps from some desire to protect them or to preserve innocence. Michael O'Loughlin discusses the difficulties associated with constructing childhood as separate from adulthood, and suggests this is a form of defence, an 'attempt to deny the unacknowledgable history of our own subjective experience and unnameable desires' (2006: 189). He draws attention to the ways we do this and hints at the cost of this separation:

> We ascribe purity of motives to children yet we create technologies of care and education that discipline their bodies and minds . . . and work to conceal from children the unconscious knowledges, especially unthought memories of trauma, that could allow children to name their histories and release their creativity.
>
> (O'Loughlin, 2006: 189)

With regularity, issues relating to the nature and maintenance of all groups were ignored, dismissed (or unseen) by the teachers. In chapter 3, the traumatic (in the psychoanalytic sense) experience of invisibility or bewilderment at the ways in which individuals were visible, was highlighted. One example of the quiet undermining of group interest was observed during an assembly. The year 6 children, who had been working with students from a local music college, performed music and songs they had composed. During one song, words of greeting from many cultures were spoken including, at one point, a Somali greeting. When this happened, two Somali girls in the class (Katie and Beyoncé) became very excited. They were clearly delighted, their faces lit up and they spoke quietly to each other. But they were immediately closed down by their teacher and told off for talking. Interestingly, the telling off was louder than whatever they had said. The incident was not mentioned later; in fact it was as if, for the teacher, it had not happened. Yet for two girls from a minority ethnic community in a school which was predominantly Bangladeshi and white-British, it had certainly happened. The rights and wrongs of talking in assembly versus listening in silence to a performance, of who can interrupt and for what reasons, are not at issue here. We just need to notice the ease with which moments of potential recognition and joining can be missed and devalued.

What holds a group together?

Both Freud and Foulkes stress the importance of libidinal ties (the degree of interest in, and commitment to, others) within the group:

> [S]pecial and dynamic relationships soon begin to form between individuals and the [leader] and between themselves, as well as between the assembly as a

whole and any of its members. Two or more factions might develop, in manifold ways. All this may be more fluctuating, or more firm and permanent.
Group members will show increasing interest in each other and consider
themselves concerned, as a whole, with what happens to any one member.
They will consider opinions, attitudes or actions, pass judgement, show tolerance or intolerance, present characteristic features, moods and reactions . . .
As soon as this little sample community shows signs of organisation and
structure in the way described, we will call it a group.

(Foulkes, 1946: 128)

I suggest the ferment of interest and activity that Foulkes notes here is strongly
disapproved of and suppressed in classrooms. Although the children's mutual
interest and excitement does get noted and talked about in staffrooms, this is most
often in terms of how to halt it. Teachers generally seek to stand apart from such
curiosity and intrigue and not to want to explore their differing relations with children in their care.

Groups, then, are structures in which I have some place, or that I choose to
reject (or that reject me). I have some notion of the boundaries of the group; that
is, what it means to belong, and consequently, what it means to be outside. The
group will fluctuate allowing the occasional admittance of a new member, and also
expel anyone deemed not to belong. Importantly, Freud suggests, it is Eros, or
love, that holds the group together; this may be love for each other or love for an
idea (a god, an injustice, a principle, etc.). While he emphasises that, as people are
complex and multi-faceted, and as we observe each other closely, libidinal ties can
be established remarkably fast (a collection of people who experience a shared
sense of peril will form a group very fast!), he is clear that 'a mere collection of
people is not a group so long as these ties have not been established in it' (Freud,
1921: 100). This implies that trying to ignore or suppress the work Foulkes
describes people doing – to make sense of each other and the groups they form –
is likely to be impossible; it may even be undesirable or counterproductive.

Defining the group

All groups, as Freud suggested, have to have some sense of what the group is: its
form, function and structure. Very often the purpose or function of groups is survival, perhaps the visceral survival that means we might be better off forming into
communities to share the growing, storing and preparation of food, child care,
defence, etc., or survival in less obvious or extreme terms. With regards to the two
girls in the assembly (mentioned earlier), maintaining an awareness of shared
Somali culture in a school in which white-British and British-Muslim cultures can,
because of their cultural or numerical superiority, afford to let things pass, might
feel just such an issue of survival. For young children, learning about who they are
is particularly important, and their explorations cover a wide range of topics

including cleverness, gender, ethnicity and so on, but also less large-scale issues. The children in Grafton School showed abiding concerns with the nature of groups, their boundaries, and issues of belonging and exclusion.

Establishing 'the untouchables'

The following incident offers an illustration of the generation of a sub-group. This group, which formed over the course of the first half of the autumn term in year 6, came together through the collusion of a small elite group of children and their teacher, Miss Warner. The children were all aware that this was the group who were top in everything that they did and who were therefore marked out for this by being seated together at a table. In an interview Frank and Karien explained the constitution of their maths group to the researcher (SC):

SC: And what do you think of your table [in maths lessons]?
Frank: It's the best table. We're with the best people [. . .] We have got our mates near us.
SC: Like Katie . . .
Karien: I sit next to Frank, Katie has her own table and Bobby sits next to Chip [. . .]
Frank: Yeah, and we're friends as well.
SC: Do you think anyone gets left out at all?
Karien: No.
SC: And how are you different to other tables?
Frank: Because all of us are in the top group for everything.
SC: So you are the smartest table?
Karien: That's what he thinks but when he said that to the teacher the teacher told him off, because she said there are much more other smart people in this class [. . .]
Frank: . . . People in the highest group are on our table, but there are some other people on other tables, but not all their tables are full of high group people.

Here, we see the construction and maintenance of a group based on the valued notions of 'ability' or 'cleverness' set up, validated and maintained by the teacher's seating arrangements. Two movements are particularly notable in this extract; the first relates to Katie, the other to the rest of the class.

Katie is undoubtedly a member of this group; the teacher's seating arrangements and her attainment in class-work and tests make this clear. She also plays football and joins in non-classroom based group activities with these boys. However, she also does not belong. There is an odd number of children in this group and so the five falls into two twos and Katie, hence 'Katie has her own table'. She sits at the group of three small tables that form the larger table, but she sits alone, no one sits next to her and she is marginalised in the group as these extracts from the field notes attest:

> They are told to work in pairs but Katie doesn't have one so she talks to an imaginary partner.
>
> (field notes)

> Miss Warner has them switch [maths test] papers so they can mark them and it causes problems that Katie has no partner to trade with. Miss Warner tells them 'it's not rocket science' and they finally sort it out.
>
> (field notes)

> The teacher asks for examples of different kinds of fractions or whole numbers ... Katie is very quick at this and she complains to her group that 'Miss always misses me.'
>
> (field notes)

While Karien was sure no one within the group was being left out, there are clearly those who are excluded and are therefore invisible to the group. A general tolerance for the peculiarities of insiders (Katie's gender for example) is, however, in marked contrast to the intolerance of outsiders:

> So long as a group formation persists or so far as it extends, individuals in the group behave as though they were uniform, tolerate the peculiarities of its other members, equate themselves with them, and have no feeling of aversion towards them.
>
> (Freud, 1921: 102)

While the teacher here is reported as telling the boys off for claiming specialness, elsewhere, and at other times, she has reinforced this view with a public naming of them as 'the untouchables'. This term, the class were told, indicated that 'no one can come near them' because their attainment or achievement was, collectively, higher than that of any other group in the class (maths and form). In labelling the group in this way and in colluding with their 'cleverness', the teacher at once set them apart as something to aspire to but, at the same time, she exposed them to the dangers of envious attacks – of hatred or envy.

Policing the boundaries

Once a group has been identified and has coalesced around some valued attributes and rules of belonging, boundaries need to be policed. This policing happens through contact with other groups which may challenge legitimacy or seek an *entrée*. Following the attack on the World Trade Center in 2001, the then president of the United States of America made it clear in a speech what exactly was at stake being friends with America at that time. Action was the price of belonging:

> A coalition partner must do more than just express sympathy, a coalition part-
> ner must perform. [. . .] Over time it's going to be important for nations to
> know they will be held accountable for inactivity. You're either with us or
> against us in the fight against terror.
>
> (Bush, 2001)

That final phrase, 'you're either with us or against us', became a defining challenge that angered as many as it appealed to, marking out both those who chose friend-ship and those that rejected it. This simplistic marking of a boundary is typical of groups and it is a pattern reiterated at all levels. Members keep each other both 'up to the mark' and not like 'the others' to make sure they all remain fit to belong. For the 'untouchables', making sure they all kept the 'cleverest' label was one impor-tant survival strategy. They often made sure they all had the right answers, supplied words and spellings for each other and guarded their chief resource – mutual help and advice – from 'outsiders'. The following examples illustrate some different 'policing' activities. In the first, the table is reasserted as a group of 'clever' children and we see a game that has been instituted within the group to keep them all loyal and on their toes:

> In the next part of the lesson they have to convert decimals into fractions.
> [. . .] Miss Warner asks the class 'Who has got it right,' and Chip answers
> 'Everyone at this table.' He has just been called 'stanky' by the rest of the
> group. I ask Katie what this means and she defers to Karien, who tells me, 'If
> you rub out last, that means you stink.' Frank adds 'It's a game we made up.'
> The game seems to be about their relational statuses as measured by their
> maths ability: anyone who doesn't keep up 'stinks'.
>
> (field notes)

While high standards of probity are required within the group, members also need to keep each other safe from attack. In the following exchange Katie risked an envious attack and was closed down by Chip:

> Finally Katie calls out 'Oh, probability!' excited that she got it. This brings her
> praise from Miss Warner but Chip mocks her for sounding too excited by
> repeating her in an overly enthusiastic tone.
>
> (field notes)

It is unclear whether this was a lesson that the untouchables were a team and none should get too ahead of the others, or whether it was about being cool and having 'effortless' knowledge, or perhaps Chip was annoyed that a girl was quicker than any of the boys, and especially himself (or some combination of these or similar reasons). But there is no doubt that he intended to shut Katie down, sending a signal to her and to others who may have heard her that the claim was made inappropriately.

However, the group's loud proclaiming of their boundaries had already been noted and reacted to. In the following exchange, Sally and Tina indicate their recognition of the boundary between the 'untouchables' and the others and, simultaneously, proclaim that they have no desire to become 'untouchables'. This was somewhat difficult for Sally who joined them for literacy (but not maths). My question followed a reference in this interview and others to the 'untouchables' and their rather bullying and excluding behaviour.

TB: Mmm … because quite a lot of people are having some difficulties with the people on that table aren't they? [yeah] Can you tell me a bit about it? [. . .] Why do you think they behave like that?
Sally: It's because they're all friends on the table.
Tina: But are you the only girl on the table?
Sally: Well, if you say that Katie is a tomboy then – yes.

To make sure she is different, Sally used Tina's assumption that only boys behave in such unacceptable ways to deny Katie, a potential ally, her femininity in a move that seems to have been ambivalent. It might be difficult to want to belong to a group that will not have you, an issue which is considered further later.

Policing can also come from without, from 'higher authorities', and some of the fragile imposed group structures leave children most anxious in this regard. The dangers that come from the teachers can be particularly brutal – falling behind with work might get one removed from a group, or, conversely, being seen to do too well can risk removal to a higher group.

A difficulty we all experience in groups comes from our experiences of intersectionality – or living in the overlaps between groups which may have rules or values which compete or conflict. The experience of being working class and academically successful is one such intersection that has been much written about (for example, Reay, 2001b). Such intersectionality is why claiming, *you're either with us or against us*, is such an unhelpful, sometimes impossible demand and why an apparently good-natured game can, in the end, fall flat:

> The game lasts a long time but it is very good-natured although, once one team has 'won', the rest claim not to have liked it so much.
>
> (field notes)

Ambivalence and groups

As mentioned earlier, there is a difficulty about being in groups. Indeed, Bion suggested that humans are group animals at war with their group nature. In saying this, he was marking the tension inherent in being simultaneously group creatures terrified by the prospect of self-loss within the group, and individuals terrified of being expelled from the safety of the group.

To belong or to shine?

The desire to be seen and to receive love is very strong in children. Freud suggests its genesis is in sibling rivalry which transforms feelings of murderous rage into a desire for justice based on the suppression of instincts:

> So there grows up in the troop of children a communal or group feeling, which is then further developed at school. The first demand made by this reaction-formation is for justice, for equal treatment for all. We all know how loudly and implacably this claim is put forward at school. If one cannot be the favourite oneself, at all events nobody else shall be the favourite. [. . .] Originally rivals, they have succeeded in identifying themselves with one another by means of a similar love for the same object.
>
> (Freud, 1921: 120)

In terms of being a group member, then, there are very real costs to be paid for membership, but, equally, for non-membership. Belonging brings with it a fear of loss of individuality and distinctiveness while the desire to be seen and loved for oneself similarly brings fears, this time of expulsion from the protective aura of the group.

Rhatul's experiences provide an illustration of this. The first two extracts come from year 5 maths lessons. Throughout the year he was very anxious and needy, wanting help and terrified that someone else might be getting more than him. This desire and fear was not peculiar to Rhatul but his extreme calling out and agitation were unusual and, in the end, did not serve him well.

> Rhatul announces to those around him 'I'm on the challenge *and* I've got everything right!' [. . .] I ask Sally about this habit and she says Rhatul is 'just boasting' and though it annoys her it 'doesn't matter'. Sophie also asserts that it doesn't matter what other people are on.
>
> (field notes)

Although Sally is somewhat sanguine about his habits here, at other times she reacted with anger and told him in no uncertain terms to shut up:

> Although Rhatul is working on his own he still seeks out interaction with his table and he asks Sally 'How about this one? 9371–2564?' He seems impressed by its level of difficulty but Sally isn't and she answers, 'How about you be quiet?'
>
> (field notes)

Unlike the experiences of 'the untouchables', here it is unclear what Rhatul is struggling to belong to; perhaps he does not know himself. It is possible he is more worried about not seeming to belong to the group of 'those who can't do it and don't know'. Those who can declare that they 'get it' or have finished can separate themselves from those that have not.

Where do children get such ideas about accomplishment? And how are they internalised by the 'losers'? Rhatul's anxiety and desperate desire to be seen as successful, and his need for love and approval from his teacher, were greater (at this point) than his need to maintain his sense of belonging to some group of peers. In year 6, however, he gradually changed, becoming quiet and subdued. His new teacher was refusing to engage with his loud jack-in-the-box persona and he was struggling to adjust. With the teacher's rejection came a wider rejection, both in the classroom and the playground:

TB: You looked really sad in the playground the other day.

Rhatul: I didn't have – today I didn't have anyone to play with . . . When I started going to my friends and say 'Can I play?' and they won't let me . . . they just won't let me. And when I go up to someone to play tennis nobody will let me . . . maybe because they already have enough children to play with . . . [And in lessons] um – like when I'm doing questions and I really want to talk to my partner and discuss it but he won't talk to me [. . .] sometimes he'll say he doesn't want me next to him 'cos he thinks I annoy him too much but I want to talk to him . . . he doesn't want to discuss it with me.

The pay-off, eventually, was ejection from the group: A difficult and painful lesson to learn and make sense of in isolation.

The desire to belong, the terror of dependency

In his essay 'Civilization and its discontents', Freud (1930) charts the development of large, cultural groups and notes how, for civilisation to develop and sustain itself, the individuals who comprise it must willingly repress some of their instincts. For us to manage to live together, murderous rages cannot be entertained, sexual desire has to be curbed, greed cannot be allowed to run riot and scarce resources must be shared. Of course, there are those who will not, or cannot, control their instincts and we have a complex system of justice which enables us to (temporarily at least) cast such people out of society (into prison) or sanctions their permanent removal (execution, deportation, etc.).

Freud identifies three sources from which he suggests all our suffering emanates: 'the superior power of nature, the feebleness of our own bodies and the inadequacy of the regulations which adjust the mutual relationships of human beings in the family, the state and society' (1930: 86). These terrors paint a vivid picture of the fears we have of our own vulnerabilities and our horror at our ultimate utter reliance on others: the power of nature to kill or maim, to inflict cold, hunger and thirst; our own mortality, the terrors of death and the unknown, of pain, suffering and loss of dignity; and that we share civilisation with those who, like nature, have powers, but with knowing minds, to hurt, kill and take advantage of our vulnerabilities. Foulkes points out that it is hardly surprising that we are afraid of the very groups that contain us. Remarking about the grand scale he says:

> It is abundantly clear that throughout all species the individual specimen is entirely unimportant and that the only thing that matters is the survival of the group and community . . . [the individual is treated] as expendable. Plans are made that literally discount millions of human lives without hesitation . . . No wonder the modern individual is afraid of the group. The individual, while helplessly compressed into a mere particle of social groups and masses, is at the same time left without any true companionship in regard to his inner mental life.
>
> (Foulkes, 1966: 152)

On a more intimate scale, Rhatul demonstrates a cost of being left out in the cold. To belong, we need to admit our vulnerabilities but we have to manage to do this in such a way that others can respond; to get help we need to ask for it in a way that can be heard, and to be seen we must expose ourselves in ways deemed acceptable by others. This is a tall order. Even so it is impossible to be known completely and so there always exists a kernel of loneliness, even within the group.

Opting out: wanting not to be part of a group

> I sent the club a wire stating, 'Please accept my resignation. I don't want to belong to any club that will accept people like me as a member'.
> Telegram to the Friar's Club of Beverly Hills to which
> he belonged, as recounted in *Groucho and Me* (Marx, 1959: 321)

One difficulty with groups is that we can sometimes feel, like Groucho Marx, that there are some we would rather not belong to. Reasons for this will vary but one danger of being part of any group is that it will demand the suppression of aspects of the self that we might otherwise enjoy. Another reason is that, in joining the group, our individuality can get lost in generalities: How can I be seen as special and worthy of love if I am just like everyone else?

It is sometimes difficult to see refusals and acts of resistance since, to avoid censure or humiliation, they are often made quietly. A playground incident reminded Sheryl, a member of the research team, that not all boys play football or fighting games, but those who don't have to keep their non-compliance with the dominant mode of masculinity somewhat quiet. During a hot summer playtime, Sheryl sought out a small patch of shade in a quiet corner of the playground. A group of boys reacted to her arrival with surprise and she noted that she initially assumed they were doing something 'naughty'. However, it soon became clear that they had simply been playing charades and were a little embarrassed. The preference for this game seemed to be something slightly covert that they shared only with each other. Apparently Sheryl as a non-school adult was not felt to be a danger to them and they got on with the game, delighting her with their acting skills and creativity and eventually inviting her to join in. For good reasons, safe spaces are often small and hard to find, even for those who would utilise them, let alone outsiders who might judge.

Taking care not to stand apart: keeping your head down

Another way to avoid the difficulties associated with being seen as an individual is to keep your head down – to make sure you are not noticed in the crowd. On several occasions girls in particular commented that they were making sure they did not do too well in some lessons as they did not want to risk being moved up a group and away from their friends. Sally was particularly anxious about this and often played down her abilities, forgoing opportunities to be noticed. In a multiplication game that the class sometimes played after maths lessons, each child had to find a place in the classroom and try to answer times table questions correctly. If they got it wrong they had to sit down but if they got it right they could take a step. If they moved close enough to anyone to touch them, then that person had to sit down. Sally preferred to settle for co-winners rather than compete; she seemed to think her best strategy was to stay put and wait it out:

> Jack guesses 64 for 6 × 9 and must sit down. Sally has wedged herself into the corner behind the desks and will only take baby steps when she gets an answer. Some of the boys try to take giant leaps to get people out, but generally aren't allowed. I ask Sally why she doesn't move out further but she tells me she has made a pact with her group that they won't tag each other, 'but it's a secret'.
>
> (field notes)

Getting subsumed, becoming invisible

While the experience of disappearing into the group can come as a relief, it can also have less desirable consequences. An incident during which Muhi was not being seen was very difficult for him to go through and for the observer to watch. During a boisterous carpet session the physical aggression among the boys turned on Muhi. Initially Jonathan, a boy with similar standing in the class to Muhi, punched him in the arm; Muhi's reaction to this was to smile. Perhaps taking the smile as an indication that the punch was okay, Chip, a more popular boy, also punched Muhi, but in the back. This time Muhi began crying but he was surrounded by the other boys and was not noticed by the teacher. Some of the children called out that he had been punched but Miss South seemed not to notice or pay attention. The researcher expected his teacher to spot his distress and to provide some comfort; certainly girls in distress always received care and attention, often including soft words and a hug. However, when she did see him crying she declared to the whole class: 'I hope Muhi isn't crying over stickers.' Jake put up his hand to tell her that Muhi had been punched but she continued with her theme: 'Well that's certainly not the way to get stickers.' Whether this was addressed to Muhi or his tormentors was ambiguous. No effort was made to discover who had caused the tears, and Muhi was left to sort out his own emotions. It seems that Muhi was expected to 'suck it up' because he was a boy. Having realised that tears did not get him the right kind of attention, another time he might try another tactic, perhaps punching back?

Feeling excluded

The experience of being excluded is common; the shifting of allegiances within classrooms can be frequent and rapid. In this chapter we have seen, however, that exclusion can come from many sources, from the larger group of peers (Rhatul), from the whole group of children and teachers (the Somali girls in assembly) and from teachers (the girl returning to her work to avoid demotion) or it can be self-chosen (the boys playing charades). The way the exclusion is experienced will depend on many things but may include depression or anger. Here Sally and Sabrina describe their fury at a teacher they experience as excluding them:

Sally: [If you feel your teacher doesn't like you] it's a bit difficult to concentrate and then she's like 'you're not concentrating properly', but then when you tell her that 'you're leaving me out' then she doesn't know how you feel because it's not happening to her!

AH: Because she's not being left out.

Sally: Yeah cos she's being, like everyone's surrounding her going Miss South, Miss South!

Sabrina: If I was Miss South yeah and Miss South was me yeah, I'd just squash her like a fly! [Laughter]

AH: What would you do Sophie?

Sophie: I'd ignore her as well.

AH: Yeah but you can't really ignore a teacher so well, it doesn't work so well that way round does it?

Sabrina: Send her to the head teacher.

Sally: I would ignore them or this is what sometimes I feel like to do with this boy in my Maths group, getting a ruler and whacking it on his head . . . yeah that's what I feel like to do with Miss South, cos teachers need things like that, especially Mrs McD . . . She needs a slap!

Conclusion

This chapter has sought to explore some of what it means to be in a group and the difficult psychic work that is required to confirm and maintain group membership. The wider educational context of the classrooms in Grafton School meant the individual was often privileged over the group and constant surveillance made it difficult to deviate from this emphasis. Emphasising the children's groups, as I have here, obscures the larger 'group-with-teacher' and also the groups that the teachers are members of.

Teachers are members of a group that requires they strive for individual achievement for all the children in their class. During our work in Grafton School, this was understood to mean that the work associated with being in a group was not something that teachers needed to concern themselves with. All such work undertaken by children was dismissed as 'fussing' or 'playing' (see also Laerke, 1998) and was relegated to the playground. But the purposes of playground groups are not the same as classroom groups; the work required in one place is not transferable to the other. Further, while children may select their playground groups, classroom groups were adult-generated and fragmented; such groups required different work.

A lot of work is done beneath the teacher's radar in all classrooms. Its easy dismissal as 'fussing' or non-compliance keeps it secret. But for groups to cohere, they need to have met those five functions: some degree of continuity; members of the group have some notion about their form and function; groups need to interact with other groups; the group should have traditions, customs and habits, especially those that give individuals a place within the group; and the group should have a definite structure.

The analysis of groups begun here has drawn on psychoanalytic theories. For Foulkes, conversation within and about a group has its parallel in the free association encouraged in individual psychoanalysis. It is in paying attention to the group's focus on itself and its members that both the group and the individuals within it can learn about and from themselves. For Foulkes, contrary to expectation, individuals tend not to get submerged in therapeutic groups, but the presence of a background brings the individual into sharper relief. Of course classrooms are not therapeutic settings (nor should they be), but being mindful that 'fuss' and 'chatting' might have a purpose seems important.

Pretending the groups are constructed 'for your own good' and that in-class ability ranking is unimportant is disingenuous. If ability grouping is not important, why do it at all? If it is important, surely it is worth enabling children to understand how it applies to them? Not all aspects of group functioning need discussing all the time, but to totally ignore or pretend these things are beneath the teacher's dignity means a lot of mental energy remains bound into the work *and* its secrecy. Making space to at least acknowledge and indicate some appreciation of the importance of the psychic group work being undertaken might free some of that energy for other purposes.

6   Group processes

Bion and the desire not to know

A person is smart. People are dumb.
(Agent K, *Men in Black*)

There is a scene in the film *Men in Black* in which Agent K (Tommy Lee Jones), inducting Agent J (Will Smith) into the agency responsible for monitoring extra-terrestrial refugees in America tells him that individuals are clever but, taken together, people are stupid. In fact, it is not so much that *en masse* people are stupid, but that thinking in groups is extremely difficult. Britzman reminds us of Freud's reasons why this might be so:

> [P]eople are susceptible to each other . . . [and] it is more difficult to think in a group than to think alone. Part of the difficulty is that the restraint or repression one might not notice when one is alone is given free-play when with others. Anxiety is contagious, and new worries can be made in groups. Another difficulty when thinking in groups is that groups tend to think in literal extremes, in exaggerations, and through an absolute splitting of good and bad, inside and outside.
>
> (Britzman, 2003: 110–11)

The psychoanalyst Wilfred Bion, however, had faith that if a group could learn to think about the fears evoked by group life – fears of vulnerability, dependency, loss, alienation, aggression and so on – then the group could provide a powerful forum for mutual learning. The problem is: that 'if' is a big one. Sustaining 'the need both to understand and develop' (Bion, 1961: 160) is far from a simple matter of concentration or will-power.

Drawing on one aspect of Bion's work, this chapter takes a closer look at uncon-scious group processes and their implications for classroom life. The focus is on the ways in which the conscious plans and desires of an individual or group can be overwhelmed and distorted by other, less 'sophisticated' concerns. For the back-ground characters in the film the desire to keep living an ordered, safe existence meant that evidence of alien life on Earth was dismissed as crankiness. The *Men in*

Black were charged with maintaining the comforting fiction, the illusion of unity and safety; they operated in secret to collude with humanity's desire not to know. In doing so, they acted as ideal 'basic assumption' leaders (see next section). The loss to humanity of not knowing about these other life-forms could not be thought about.

For teachers, evidence of groups' difficulties with thinking can be particularly clear at times of stress – in the run-up to exams for example, when otherwise motivated and organised learners regress to neediness and insecurity. At times like these, teachers can feel themselves being pushed to 'give in' and provide answers, to take a more overtly parental role to allay concerns and to promise that all will be well. Yet Freud warns educators against overprotecting the young. In failing to enable them to think about the difficulties and disappointments they may face, 'education is behaving as though one were to equip people starting on a Polar expedition with summer clothing and maps of the Italian Lakes' (Freud, 1930: 134). His suggestion is that to act in this way is to refuse an ethical dimension of one's task as an educator – a serious allegation.

Groups complicate and confuse the learning environment. But they are inescapable, which means that the complications and confusions they create are also inescapable; we cannot simply wish them away:

> Group psychology . . . invokes the very conditions for becoming an individual, and part of becoming an individual means worrying about the loss of distinction, the worthiness of one's subjective insistences, and the uncertain meanings of dependency beyond childhood.
>
> (Britzman, 2003: 107)

Once brought together into groups by institutions (classes, cohorts, departments, etc.), people start to select and develop sub-groups of their own: friendship groups, groups based on ethnicity, gender, 'attractiveness', 'cleverness' and so on. These sub-groups may make more sense to individuals than the larger educational group or may meet different needs. For example, while I may be taught in the chemistry class, my friendship with the few other girls in the room helps me maintain a sense of my femininity in the overwhelmingly masculine environment of the lab. My sense of femininity is a more immediate and pressing concern than the chemistry exam next year: this task makes more 'human' sense to me at the moment and in this context than my long-term career. As we have seen, children in school (like anyone) work hard to develop and maintain their sub-groups, and the kinds of work they undertake have been widely discussed.

Much of the maintenance work that groups undertake (discussed in chapter 5) is typically pushed aside by teachers in schools and relegated to the playground; it is not part of the approved curriculum of the classroom. Paradoxically, the more teachers seek to control the agenda of the classroom by rejecting groups' maintenance work, the more threatened group members may feel and the more they will turn to other groups for reassurance, potentially building a cycle of apparent 'non-compliance' in the classroom.

Wilfred Bion and the basic assumption groups

This chapter explores group processes and the experience of being placed in the position of 'leader' under what Bion called 'basic assumption' conditions. Bion's theories, initially developed from work with shell-shocked soldiers during the Second World War, were extended in his later clinical work with adults in therapeutic groups. Subsequent to Bion's original work, the notion of the basic assumption and working groups has been used across a wide variety of settings including organisations (Jaques, 1984; Nitsun, 1996).

In his book *Experiences in Groups*, Bion (1961) presents and develops his ideas about groups. His suggestion is that the first and most basic concern of a group is with its survival: its 'basic assumption' is that it is under threat and until it is convinced that it is not, no work, other than ensuring survival, can take place. Once its anxieties have been contained and it feels secure enough, the group can begin to take on other, less vital, ('work') tasks. For this reason, Bion suggests, groups experience different emotional states. These states tend to oscillate between the desirable 'working group' state in which 'work' tasks can be undertaken, and less desirable 'basic assumption' states in which the anxious need to ensure survival dominates. While an individual within a group may have good conscious intentions, the group state of being will generally override these; that is to say, unconscious group processes tend to out-weigh conscious individual wishes. General class concerns about an impending deadline will tend to overwhelm individual questions or more general discussions about aspects of course content. This troubling of our desire to be agentic individuals can evoke resistant responses, especially a desire to deny the influence of the group so that we may fail to acknowledge occasions when a group concern overwhelms an individual desire. For example, if we are all worried about the way our essays will be received (by the teacher's mind when she marks them) then a discussion about key concepts that I might be able to incorporate into my essay is much less desirable than the teacher, yet again, describing the literal way the essays will be received within the department: the hand-in procedures and assessment processes.

Bion suggests that all groups come together for a purpose and that this purpose may be more or less clear to any one member of the group at different times. Some groups come together mindfully although even they may subsequently lose focus, with the overt purpose being overwhelmed by a need to survive the experience of being together in this situation now. That is, conscious processes can be overwhelmed by unconscious anxieties and, when unconscious anxieties overwhelm conscious intentions, unconscious defences take over.

When a committee meets it generally has an agenda, a shared common purpose that brings with it tasks to be completed (items on the agenda to be discussed, actions to be agreed upon and allocated). So long as the group is able to maintain its 'sophisticated' or 'working' structure, it will stay in touch with reality and its objectives will, to some extent at least, be met. However, the forces acting against the maintenance of this structure are legion. Manifestations of things going wrong include: one member of the committee drifting off or even falling asleep, perhaps missing something important or requiring a recap; the committee may distract itself with its annoyance at the absence (again!) of members felt to be key; large sections of the membership may get caught up in a suggestion made and explored by two members who then need to go away and develop it and bring it back (it'll save so much time in the long run); or a row might erupt and the committee dissolve into chaos unless someone can bring it back to order/ sophistication.

These familiar examples of a committee struggling to fulfil its task at a given moment illustrate Bion's notion of basic assumption groups. The 'basic assumption' here is that the group is under threat and needs to survive. Any more sophisticated structure has to be able to endure the anxieties evoked by the threat and subsequent protective basic assumption structure. Bion suggests that there are three main ways the group can ensure its survival:

- by looking for a leader to keep them safe and provide protection (basic assumption dependency),
- by looking for a leader to lead them into battle or to safety (basic assumption fight/flight), or
- by looking to two people to provide a saviour (basic assumption pairing).

These basic assumptions can emerge unconsciously in any group; each develops out of different threats and therefore looks for different kinds of salvation. These groups, like all others, are neither static nor stable. At any moment, sub-groups within a large group may be operating under different basic assumptions and basic assumptions can fluctuate rapidly or may endure for considerable periods.

It is important to bear in mind that the emergence of a basic assumption is not a deliberate, rational act; it is the very opposite. The emergence of a basic assumption within a group is an unconscious reaction to anxiety, to fears of real or imagined threats to the survival of the group. Therefore bringing a group back to sophistication/work requires the unconscious anxieties be addressed in a way that can be experienced as sincere and believable. There is an important distinction here between the overt, speakable anxiety, for example a fear that one will not do oneself justice in a test, and an unconscious anxiety that is not speakable, maybe that one is not loveable (and therefore not worthy of learning and doing well in tests). Telling a group they will do fine because they have covered the curriculum appears to address the overt anxiety but may not address the unconscious one.

It is not possible to directly address unconscious anxieties. The need in some way to do so is part of what makes education an impossible profession – how can one answer an unconscious/unknowable demand? The simple answer is that one cannot, yet these unknowable demands wield influence insistently. Attending to the impacts of the anxieties of others is therefore an unending imperative; ignoring them will not make them go away. How then can one be a 'good-enough' teacher? If these anxieties cannot be ignored or directly addressed, can they perhaps be contained?

A consideration of basic assumption states can help us to think about group behaviours. There is no simple recipe for dealing with any of these but they can provide a useful point for reflection on the kind of leadership that is being demanded and whether this is the kind of leader we want to be. Or, if we find ourselves in the group, Bion's basic assumptions can help us think about the demands we are making of others and what these may tell us about our own learning needs. All three basic assumptions are described below although, in what follows, the basic assumption dependent group will be the main focus.

Dependent groups

The dependent group looks for someone who can solve their difficulties without the group having to make any effort; perhaps a teacher who can do the learning for them. The main demand is that the person they depend on, their 'saviour', should behave like an ideal parent and provide security. Bion cites religious groups who turn to the (mother) Church and/or God (the father), as examples of dependent groups operating on a societal scale. The task of the basic assumption dependent group then is to make sure that each group member and the group as a whole are worthy of redemption. However, members of the dependent group may feel themselves to be inadequate to the task. Painful feelings of emptiness and frustration demand an omnipotent or omniscient other who can meet the terrible demand of their needs for knowing and understanding. The group unconsciously assumes that some sort of magic resides in the leader so that they can know all the group's unbearable needs without these having to be articulated.

In learning groups of this kind, students frequently direct attention to the tutor's remarks, as if they were the source of all wisdom, to the exclusion of their peers' contributions. They may insist that the teacher become a particular kind of (often authoritarian) leader even if this is not the way the teacher would like to operate. Even if learners lose respect for a particular tutor there is a sense in which the position is endowed with authority, or at least that there is some external power which determines what should be learned whether or not the tutor is the medium. This external authority might be the curriculum documents, the official 'scheme of work', exam syllabus or published text books. Tasks not directly related to these sources are deemed to be valueless and, while they may be completed, they are simultaneously rejected.

Feeling unworthy of redemption may seem a strange suggestion in relation to learning. Within a classroom, the difficulty of accepting knowledge and of feeling worthy of the teacher's good attentions can generate difficult feelings of guilt. Bion suggests that, in demanding the attention he needs, a student 'is being greedy in demanding more than his fair share of parental care' (Bion, 1961: 74); he may feel he is taking the teacher away from someone else who needs that attention more. Similarly, people who struggle to accept their capacity to learn can be incredulous when they receive affirmation: 'I still can't believe I passed my exam.' Perhaps more difficult, or more familiar, is the experience of sitting in a class feeling overwhelmed by the task of learning, feeling empty and hopeless (I'll *never* get this), being incapable of putting your hand up to ask for help and wishing the teacher would slow down, repeat something, *see* the agony and misery on your face, or that *someone* would put their hand up only to discover during a break that everyone was apparently sitting feeling the same thing. Why did no one speak up?

A basic assumption dependent group, demanding endless explanations and reassurance, wanting to be known and understood without effort, and begging to be spoon-fed can be very frustrating to work with. Placed in a parental role, the teacher can become infuriated; the group needs to 'grow up'. Realistic advice may be sage but it is not the advice that is desired and the group will return incessantly to its theme to provoke the answer it wants. But, like the very young infant, learners experience ambivalence around being parented: we want it, but at the same time we do not, it can feel restrictive. Even a good parent will be fought since, following Klein, parenting brings both the 'good', sustaining breast and 'bad', persecuting breast. In demanding a parental reaction the basic assumption dependency group is the most straightforward response to anxiety. But it is not enough. As Bion noted:

> If the desire for security were all that influenced the individual then the dependent group might suffice, but the individual needs more than security for himself and therefore needs other kinds of group. If the individual were prepared to suffer the pains of development, and all that that implies on efforts to learn, he might grow out of the dependent group. But the fact that he wishes, even with the impulses that are not satisfied in the dependent group, for a state in which, without undergoing the pains of growth, he could be fully equipped for group life, results in a pull towards a group structured for pairing or for fight/flight.
>
> (1961: 91)

Pairing groups

Often this basic assumption forms when the group is bored, lost or resentful and is unable to express or otherwise cope with these feelings. Perhaps when we are 'bored to death' only new life can save us. In a pairing group, two people are 'nominated' to form a pair whose 'offspring' or 'brainchild' will save the group from its failings. Bion suggested that at a societal level the aristocracy fulfil this hope, although that may be a suggestion that is more difficult to work with now than it was in the UK in the 1950s. Basic assumption pairing is in evidence when there is some expectation that a solution to all the difficulties will emerge out of some magical happening that takes place elsewhere: the 'birth' of a new idea, a conversation, the work of a different group (including the cleaners, a builder, a task group, etc.). In learning groups, pairing can take three possible forms. Jaques (1984) illustrates these with familiar examples:

- Two students provide mutual respect and support for each other to the exclusion of other members of the group who are left with nothing to do; the pair takes over.
- The pair may indulge in intellectual battle, each partner representing a different side of a conflict that has been preoccupying the group. Again, the rest of the group are mere bystanders.
- The tutor may pair with the group as a whole and collude with them in their wish to avoid work.

He goes on to explain that pairing is often characterised by a sense of unreal hope:

> 'Everything will be okay when we get a new room', 'It'll come all right after Christmas'. The need to face up to and work through disappointments and failures is conveniently avoided by this unreal but seductive promise of things to come.
>
> (Jaques, 1984: 16)

Once the new conditions are met – the new classroom is ready, the spring term has started – there can be a terrible sense of disappointment that the magic has not worked.

Fight/flight groups

Here, the group seeks to preserve itself from annihilation either by attacking something (*fight*) or by avoiding the task (*flight*). Bion suggests that the army provides an example of this basic assumption working at a societal level. In more intimate contexts, the forms of attack are unlikely to be physical although they can be no less savage for that:

> Commonly the group will scapegoat (*fight*) some other person or group in order to avoid a difficult problem. *Flight* on the other hand takes the form of withdrawal, passivity, dwelling in the past or jesting. The group seems happy to distract itself from its task by focussing on some other harmless and irrelevant issue. 'In this move, the group uses its energy to defend itself from its

own internal fears and anxieties, and consequently neither develops nor achieves an effective output' (de Board, 1978).

(Jaques, 1984: 15, emphasis in the original)

As Bion notes this group assumes (or generates) someone or something to fight or run away from and this can be the official leader/teacher (1961: 67). If the teacher is the one to be escaped from, a class may collude with a peer's non-compliant behaviour to keep the teacher (and/or the learning they embody) embattled and at a distance; this scenario forms the basis of many teacher nightmares. A difficulty is the need to consider *why* the class perceives the teacher to be the threat. In this kind of situation, reasserting control can become a battle of wills, but taking a confrontational route might confirm the class's belief that the teacher is the source of the threat.

Convoluted and uncomfortable though it may be, when some group we are in fails to make the progress it thinks it should, and we start to blame some other group for distracting us, what we may need to do is face the delightful distraction we find in the existence of these others. In this situation, where one group focusses on another and distracts itself with blaming games, Bion might suggest they are acting on a fight/flight basic assumption. A key question might be, not, 'How can we get rid of our annoyance?', but, 'Why are we looking for distraction?'

A warning against systematicity and transference

It is not uncommon for a teacher to collude with a group's basic assumption, for example, their desire not to have to face up to a subject they are failing in or find threatening. Chapter 4 briefly considered Muhi's confusion at having been moved down into Miss Middleton's mathematics group where no mathematics took place. His impression of the class was corroborated by other children who spoke of this teacher's mathematics class as a safe, if somewhat non-mathematical, environment:

Sally: For maths I'm in Miss Middleton's group and she doesn't really like teaching maths so she takes us to [where the computers are] and we do fun stuff. Sometimes her maths is doing fun stuff like colouring in and painting masks.

Miss Middleton stated repeatedly and publicly that she did not like, and was not good at, mathematics. It is possible to read her avoidance of the subject as her forming a pair with the group to avoid the difficult feelings that mathematics evoked for them all (together they might generate other activities to ward off the maths) or to think of it as her leading the group in flight from the task of learning. Perhaps both are true? Her reaction to teaching the 'least able' group provides us with an example of the difficulty of trying to use Bion's basic assumptions as a tool with which to 'fix' problem groups. Typologies hold out the (false) promise of a system that may enable us to control our own anxieties about teaching groups who seem not to want to learn. But, paradoxically, employing systematicity to 'fix' a problem is a defence (Bass, 1998) and a way to escape the difficulty of having to think about what is going on. Despite these problems, it does seem that having some understanding of the structure and desires of basic assumption groups, while not a recipe for rescue, might provide a tool for thought and reflection; a way of responding less reactively and more mindfully.

Miss Middleton's behaviour, her (incorrect) belief that everyone in her group felt the same way about mathematics as she did, reminds us of the need to act reflexively in the classroom. This demand is difficult. Staying with Miss Middleton, we can see that it is possible that she might be replaying her own difficult mathematics learning experiences in her interactions with the 'low ability' mathematics group. Perhaps being with this group causes her to re-experience her own mathematical learning and conjures up her own, old inabilities (real or imagined). This new edition of an old conflict (Freud, 1899) is an example of transference, or an unconscious defence that enables learning not to take place. Pitt and Britzman explain that transference is a process 'where one makes sense of new situations through the imperatives of older conflicts' (2003: 759). What is 'forgotten' by the teacher in the throes of this defence is that she and the student are not the same person (Britzman and Pitt, 1996: 120).

It is of course possible that Miss Middleton believed she was acting kindly and with empathy in protecting her maths group from difficult encounters with mathematics. But the line between empathy and acting out in the transference is a fine one. Freud considers the difficulty of empathy:

> We shall always tend to consider people's distress objectively – that is, to place ourselves, with our own wants and sensibilities, in *their* conditions, and then to examine what occasions we should find in them for experiencing happiness or unhappiness. This method of looking at things, which seems objective because it ignores the variations in subjective sensibility, is, of course, the most subjective possible, since it puts one's own mental states in the place of any others, unknown though they may be.
>
> (Freud, 1930: 89, emphasis in the original)

As Frosh notes, 'unconscious feelings from the past dictate irrational responses to the present' (2002: 89). For a teacher to assume that students do not want to learn seems to be an irrational act. And, unfortunately, Frosh suggests, 'transference is an escalating phenomenon: once the self imposes it on the other, it tends to create its own reality, so that the other comes to act in line with what the self expects' (Frosh, 2002: 90). In this way, Muhi was in the process of struggling to make sense of the way he was being constructed in his new mathematics group. It seems possible that he would learn to live down to Miss Middleton's expectations.

In reflecting on the difficulty of being a leader to a group (including one acting under a basic assumption), Bion suggests that it is important to be able to refigure an experience. That is, to be able to think about its 'reverse and obverse' and its 'dual' (1961: 89); to think not only about what one has experienced, to think about resonances this has in one's biography and what those resonances might tell you, but also to think about how the group might be responding and the kinds of res-onances that might be set up for them, *and* any parallel examples that have similar-ities in structure or nuance. This is a tall order and a far cry from simple exhortations to reflective practice aimed at evaluating and improving practice such as 'how did my lesson go today?' and 'who learned what?' (for further discussion of this see Moore, 2004).

Cheating in the dependent maths group?

During observations of mathematics lessons in the autumn term of year 5, I often sat with the same group of boys: Houssain, Rhatul, Muhi, Matthew and Shanhrul. Over time, I became aware of how anxious the boys seemed during these lessons. This manifested itself in a variety of ways. For Houssain and Rhatul in particular there was a lot of nervous twitching, fidgeting, lots of joking and noisy demands for my attention: 'Is this right? Is this right?' Muhi also did this but to a much lesser extent. Matthew watched and listened attentively as the others expressed anxiety. Perhaps unable to join in, he nevertheless was very much involved with the group's distractions. The one who seemed to have the most mathematical understanding was Shanhrul. For example, faced with questions such as 'how many 7s in 28?', while the rest of the group struggled to draw tallies to count out answers, he quickly realised that he could use the multiplication tables stuck high on the class-room walls. His anxiety seemed more about the way things were written and set out than about the mathematics itself. For Shanhrul, my presence seemed calming and he was able to use me to learn; for the others, my presence sometimes seemed to escalate their anxiety.

During one observation, I was particularly struck by the way Rhatul and Houssain responded to my sitting next to Shanhrul. Shanhrul talked to me a lot and checked ideas with me, asking 'Is it like this?' or 'Can I do it this way?' rather than 'Is this right?' During the lesson, we compared, as we had before, different ways of working, and talked about the merits and problems of different solution strategies. On this occasion, Rhatul got very upset and protested to the group that Shanhrul was cheating because I was 'telling him the answers'. The atmosphere eventually became rather unpleasant with Shanhrul becoming embarrassed and Rhatul's tone growing increasingly aggressive. Eventually I asked him to come and talk to me (rather than shouting at me across the table).

As Rhatul crept sheepishly around the table and with the others watching intently, I realised I had stopped being a 'researcher' and had become a 'teacher'. It was clear he thought I was going to tell him off; I didn't. I commented that his behaviour was not very helpful, that Shanhrul and I were talking about division and that he was welcome to join in if he would find that useful, but that shouting across the table was just rather distracting. I pointed out that Shanhrul had had some interesting ideas. Rhatul became much quieter after this and did join in with working through a calculation together at the end of the lesson.

In other contexts, cheating can mean using subterfuge to bend or break the rules to win or gain unfair advantage. It suggests taking advantage of a situation to 'put one over' on others who are engaged in the same competition for some resource or prize. In relation to mathematics, cheating can take many forms. Actions such as copying an answer are labelled cheating but so are other, less obvious examples such as using a 'trick' to get an answer with less effort than others. I am sure that my telling Shanhrul the answers would count as cheating but I was not doing that. My sense was that the rest of the group could not bear the thought that anyone was getting help they were not: the thought that someone might want to talk about methods appeared to be unthinkable. It was clear that cheating was a huge issue for these boys and they were unable to use me as a resource for learning. 'Cheating' was a term that enabled them to talk about feeling robbed of love/attention/teaching. They chose to turn Shanhrul's 'greedy' discussions into an excuse to protest at my presence. While Rhatul made most of the running in these protestations, it was clear that the others agreed with his complaints.

Bion's insights make some of these dynamics less surprising:

> The dependent group, with its characteristic elevation of one person, makes difficulties for the ambitious, or indeed for anyone who wishes to get a hearing, because it means that in the eyes of the group, and of themselves, such people are in a position of rivalry with the leader. Benefit is felt no longer to come from the group, but from the leader of the group alone, with the result that individuals feel they are being treated only when [they are] talking to the leader of the group. This leads to a sense – the more unpleasant since it is associated with asking too much and giving too little – that they are being cheated or starved.
>
> (Bion, 1961: 79)

We could therefore read this incident as one in which Rhatul and his peers feel 'starved', as my attention was with Shanhrul and their teacher's was elsewhere. The noisy clamour certainly made it hard for Shanhrul, or anyone else, 'to get a hearing'. The noise also pushed me into taking 'adult' and teacher-like action: I singled Rhatul out and asked him to come to me. The group had created the leader it needed and in the moment at which I appeared to take on the role of a basic assumption dependent leader the atmosphere changed. By not conforming to expectations (I did not tell anyone off or insist on quiet working) I failed to behave like a basic assumption leader – it may be for that reason that for a few minutes, the group managed to work together on some mathematics.

Being a leader

One of the difficulties of basic assumption groups is that they *demand* leaders that behave in particular ways, ways we might want either to collude with or reject. However, in either colluding with or rejecting the assigned role, we are in danger of enabling the group to remain in a basic assumption mode, when what we might intend is to move it to a 'sophisticated' or 'working' group structure.

Let us imagine ourselves faced with a group of students who have had repeated experiences of failing to learn. To add insult to injury they have now been distilled into a small 'nurture group' and been put in our care so that they can have opportunities to 'learn at their own level' and so 'catch up' with the 'better' learners. Perhaps unsurprisingly the group is resentful, angry and resistant. By turns they want us to give them the answers, listen to their endless grievances and make sure they never fail again. Individuals take on the roles of clown and chief moaner. Perhaps with relief we recognise one or two who do want to learn so we can focus our good teaching/feeding on them and try to ignore the others who distract and disrupt. This is perhaps how Rhatul and Houssain interpreted my interaction with Shanhrul during the mathematics lesson.

Paradoxically, *either* colluding with *or* rejecting whatever it is that they want maintains the anxious state since the anxiety has been neither identified nor addressed. The group's aim, in a basic assumption state, is to survive intact – at an unconscious level it does not want its anxieties addressed, as that would challenge and change the group. The double bind is that, even as it frustrates and angers individuals to be labelled as not-knowing, the comfortable, familiar place for the individuals and the group is precisely the one in which they do not know. Basic assumption groups do not tolerate activities that do not serve their aims. Leaders who refuse to lead in the desired way are hard to understand and the group may struggle to 'hear' them: the leader who will not take the difficulties away, the leader who will not lead the attack or flight, the leader who insists that the whole group engage are all (to the group) bad leaders.

Bion's writing provides important lessons for those 'elected' to be leaders of basic assumption groups. The first of these is that the fear and anxiety in the group needs to be made the problem of the group, not the problem of individuals, whether that be the teacher or individual learners. Rhatul's anxious calling out in the maths group was not only about *his* anxiety, although his was certainly the most evident. Using Bion as a tool for reflection we can see that shouting at him would only have elevated his anxiety and, deprived of their proxy-outlet, the anxieties of the rest of the group. Drawing the rest of the group into a discussion about cheating and collaboration might have helped them to understand that all of them had concerns and that all of them (together) could reach a solution. They did not need to rely on me for judgements about the mathematics; Shanhrul could help them too, if they would trust him and if he could accept and respond positively to the responsibility. Insights such as this offer the possibility of changing the way a teacher might behave with such a group.

However, attempts to get the group to take responsibility for itself are likely to engender feelings of persecution and increase the demand for a *really* strong leader who will sort everything out, who will know what to do, and who, above all, will act. Bion's description of his work with soldiers at Northfields Hospital includes some examination of what happened when he refused to make everything okay for the men. Rather than setting up routines that might have been expected from an army hospital, Bion created an environment in which the men were expected to plan their own time. Apart from a daily parade, used somewhat like a school assembly, the men had only a few rules. Translating these into school-type terms:

- everyone had to do an hour's physical education a day (unless they had a medical certificate),
- everyone had to go to one or more class from those on offer,
- anyone could form a new class if there wasn't one he liked the look of or if the one he wanted to join was unable to take him,
- if anyone was unable to go to class they had to go to the rest-room which was overseen by someone who would maintain it as a place of quiet (nothing above a whisper) and log everyone's names.

Despite these conditions, designed to encourage the men to take responsibility for their actions, things did not start well. The opportunity to take responsibility and behave as 'grown-ups' able to take decisions about their time (rather than dependent children in need of parenting) was strongly resisted:

> Although there were many groups and almost entire freedom to each man to follow the bent of his own inclinations, provided he could make a practical proposal, yet very little was happening . . . it almost looked as if the training wing was a façade with nothing behind it. This, I said [during the parade], seemed odd because I remembered how bitterly the patients in the training wing had complained to me that one of their objections to the army was the 'eyewash'. Its presence in the training wing, therefore, really did seem to be a point worth study and discussion. This announcement left the audience looking as if they were being 'got at'.
>
> (Bion, 1961: 17)

Bion refused to be turned into an obvious army leader, and a change did come about as the men started to take responsibility for themselves and their environment. Despite this, however, he explained that:

Men began to complain to me that patients were taking advantage of the laxity of the organisation. 'Only 20 per cent', they said, 'of the men are taking part and really working hard; the other 80 per cent are just a lot of shirkers'. They wanted such men to be punished, or otherwise dealt with.

(Bion, 1961: 18–19)

His men expected Bion to take responsibility for sorting it out. This description always makes me smile; it is very familiar to me as a teacher. Set to work collaboratively, one or two members of a group will often claim that they have 'done all the work'. Indeed, observing groups there always seem to be some who are happy to let others graft; similarly, there will be those whose contribution is not recognised. And always, there are those who claim they are being taken advantage of, who feel persecuted by their 'lazy' peers and want the teacher to *do something* about it.

Insisting that the difficulty – the disorganisation, the ignorance, the desire not to have to learn – be made a problem of the group rather than a problem of the teacher and/or a problem of the non-compliant 80 per cent, is a radical move. Suggesting the group look to itself, pointing out their resistances, may not be welcome, especially if this draws the group's attentions to its basic assumptions, perhaps that the teacher knows everything or can know what the students need without being told. Groups may become angry and resentful, emotions designed to provoke the desired response: that the teacher/leader fulfil their basic assumption role and lead. And in this, they are usually very effective!

A second lesson we can draw from Bion's work relates to the way teachers think about groups of learners. As teachers we need to think not only about what we have said and done but also about what the group thinks we have said and done. The focus needs to be on the ways people believe others see and react to them as well as what might have been intended. The episode of 'cheating' described earlier is unusual in that I observed it as a researcher. I had the time and space to sit repeatedly with that group of boys and to watch their interactions and their learning over a period of weeks. I am sure that, had I been the class's teacher, I would have been driven to distraction by the sheer volume (quantity *and* noise level) of Rhatul's explosions. An easy 'reflective' reading of the group's behaviour would be that the tasks were too difficult for them and so the challenge needed to be reduced. And indeed, this is what happened. Over time most of them – including Shanhrul – ended up in a lower maths group – although we are perhaps beginning to see that this might not be a necessary or a desirable outcome.

It is the nature of group processes that they *are* hard to think about not least because there is no place to stand outside them. Bion, reflecting on his own role, describes it well:

[T]he emotional situation is nearly always tense and confused, so that it is not always easy for the psychiatrist, who must necessarily be a part of the group, to tell what is going on. Feelings of frustration are common, boredom is acute, and often relief is provided only by outbursts of exasperation between members of the group.

(Bion, 1961: 59)

The field notes from the project are full of comments about our difficulties, as researchers, in thinking about what might have been happening or our experiences of boredom and distraction that seemed at one with the mood of the class. Sometimes the children themselves demonstrated insight. For example, after a particularly rowdy and unproductive rehearsal for the class's Christmas play had been abandoned, a member of the research team asked a group of children why they thought everyone had been so 'excited'. Yasmin, recognising a connection between rowdy uncontrollability and anxiety, suggested that it might be because everyone was so nervous about performing the play. Yet although it seems obvious once the thought had been voiced, the terrors of performance had not been raised by teachers or pupils.

A final lesson, and one Bion struggled with himself, is that the 'grown-up' (the teacher/psychiatrist/whoever) does not always have the answer and cannot lead the group away from their difficulties. This is part of the constitutive difficulty of teaching and learning. The difficult task of the 'adult' is to enable the group to face its difficulties and to learn from them. Despite the difference in rank and 'health', Bion steadfastly refused to become the desired dependent leader in the hospital; he did not have answers or cures. It is not that he shirked responsibility; his leadership seems to have been considered and he evidently stood staunchly between the men and the officials on the army board who wanted them turned around and sent back to the front lines as quickly as possible.

Such a response is very much about thinking through what leadership might mean. While the official 'primary task' of Northfields Hospital was 'fixing' men so they could be sent back to fight, Bion considered his task to be enabling the men to reintegrate into civilian society and become active citizens again. This meant providing them with opportunities not to blindly follow orders. The definitions of 'health' were very different. Perhaps, as teachers faced with group processes, we need to make a distinction between government or policy notions of 'education' as the technical and rational acquisition of skills towards employability, and other, broader definitions of being educated and learning; choices between magical 'parental', intuitive responses to learners and other, more considered, mindful responses?

Conclusion

By our immersion in groups, and our susceptibility to other people, 'we are constantly affected by what we feel to be the attitude of a group to ourselves, and are consciously or unconsciously swayed by our idea of it' (Bion, 1961: 32). The teacher, like the psychoanalyst, has an ethical responsibility to think about the issues raised by a consideration of group processes. To react impulsively to the demands of groups acting under a basic assumption (and that is most groups most of the time) is to maintain the unconscious anxieties that generated that state of mind in the first place. And if the energy in the group is directed to short-term survival then it cannot attend to the slower processes of learning.

The three basic assumption groups that Bion described can help us to act more mindfully. Although they cannot 'cure' problem groups, they can help us to think through the ways we feel we are being encouraged to act. Finding ourselves colluding with – or fighting against – requests to simplify tasks, with distractions that take our focus elsewhere, with fantastical hopes and wishes, can all alert us to the existence of unconscious anxieties. While we may respond to these requests automatically in the heat of the moment, taking time to think reflexively, in that more complex way that Bion suggested, can help us not to react so predictably the next time or to revisit an incident with a group in a discussion. It is unhelpful to think in terms of blame. These behaviours are not planned; they are unconscious responses to affects aroused by uncertain elements in the (internal and external) environment. Whether by omission or commission, we are complicit in them since we are part of the group.

Reflexivity moves us beyond a need to reflect on experiences and lessons. Reflection concerns itself with systems and procedures: 'Who learned what?', 'Did my planning enable all the groups to engage with the task?' and these are important questions. But, as Moore points out:

> Reflexivity moves the . . . practitioner *beyond* such forms of self-evaluation towards its location . . . in a much bigger picture: a picture that may include the practitioner's own history, dispositions, prejudices and fears, as well as the wider social, historical and cultural contexts in which schooling itself is situated. In other words, within *reflexivity*, that which is reflected upon . . . is not treated as if it were the whole picture, but is made sense of with reference to what is happening in the rest of the larger picture.
>
> (Moore, 2004: 149, emphasis in the original)

Such a turn would enable 'both learning about an experience, culture, or event, and learning from one's own reading of an experience, culture or event' (Britzman and Pitt, 1996: 119). Bion highlights the folly of thinking that group processes can be ignored or that difficulties associated with reflexive thinking can be avoided:

> If an individual claims he has no doubt at all [about the reasons for the behaviour of a group], one would really like to know why not. Are there occasions when the group attitude is utterly unmistakable? Or is the individual unable to tolerate ignorance about a matter in which it is essential to be accurate if his behaviour in a society is to be wise?
>
> (Bion, 1961: 45)

Acts of reflexivity need to encompass a move not only to the broader complexities of the educational context but also to the complexities submerged by ideas like 'the class' and colluded with in the notion that the teacher and the class, the knower and the learner, are static and clearly identifiable positions. There is always another position from which to observe what is happening and which might subtly shift the relations between all involved.

7 When does the lesson start?

Thoughts, thinking, learning
and knowing

The previous chapter illustrated how a focus on the defensive basic assumption group (dependency, pairing and fight/flight) made it difficult to maintain a focus on the working group. The 'sophisticated' structure of the working group is characterised by a belief that the effort of work is necessary and worthwhile. Such a belief is perhaps exemplified by teachers' exhortations that their students 'think about it', as if thinking were entirely under conscious control. Bion explains that particular ideas are important to the existence of the working group:

> [T]he idea of 'development' rather than 'full equipment by instinct' [is] an integral part of [the working group], but so is the idea of a rational or scientific approach to problem solving. So also, as an inevitable concomitant of the idea of 'development', is accepted the validity of learning by experience.
>
> (Bion, 1961: 99)

These conditions, particularly a recognition and toleration of the need to develop and to learn mindfully from experience, represent issues that are equally difficult for individuals and groups. Such behaviour presumes a capacity to think – and what is education if it is not about thinking, or perhaps learning to think?

But if we are asked to say what we are thinking, or to say something about what it means to think or how we think, such questions may seem very hard, perhaps impossible to answer. Talking about thinking is wrapped up in talk about knowing and not knowing. Our language slips and slides, bouncing us around thoughts, ideas, concepts, notions, flashes of insight and pits of empty-headedness until we either manage something that somehow does not quite capture whatever it was we thought we wanted to say, or we are left stuttering in a storm of inarticulacy.

In a recent BBC documentary for the Horizon television series, the mathematician Professor Marcus de Sautoy reflected on a moment when he realised he knew something. He began by explaining that it is his job to solve problems but that he is stumped by his own creative thought processes: he does not know how he comes to know. Indeed, disconcertingly, knowing appears to come from not thinking:

> Twenty years ago I was making the same [train] journey I am now [. . .] and what happened on that journey really changed my life. I was really stuck on this thorny problem, I'd been stuck on it for months and I was getting nowhere with it and suddenly this flash came into my head. It was like a flash of electricity and I suddenly saw how to crack this problem. Everything became clear in that moment. It was such a rush of adrenalin, realising that I'd cracked this problem that I'd been working on. Ever since I've wanted to know, where do those ideas come from? I want more of them. And it somehow just came from gazing out of the window thinking about nothing – I thought.
>
> (de Sautoy, 2009)

The programme went on to explore the biomechanics of the brain, not a route pursued here. But his amazement, vividly conveyed, at the surprise realisation that he suddenly 'had it' is familiar. Indeed, the experience of a Eureka! or 'penny-dropping' moment is so familiar and satisfying to us that it has recently been used to advertise teaching as a career to graduates. Of course, de Sautoy had thought about his 'thorny problem' and had done years of work on and around it but however much his conscious mind had engaged, some kernel had eluded him. In the end, the result came about in an apparently magical moment, and any sense of process vanished. The effort appeared to have disappeared, there was no mighty lever there at the final moment prising the knowledge away from the ignorance. So, again we might ask: What is this process of thinking? What is it to come to know?

There are any number of rational explanations of thinking; philosophers and cognitive psychologists have generated shelves and shelves of descriptions, narratives and theories. But, like de Sautoy, I find myself doing battle with the rationalist fantasy that thought is the product of thinking; that is, that thoughts are somehow constructed from, woven out of, or emerge from the act of thinking. So tidy. But I know when I have been working on a problem, when I have been thinking, what emerges is often so much less than I started with. Bits of idea have fallen away, been forgotten. The end result may be satisfying, an elegant solution, a beautiful and unexpected conjunction, but the forgotten parts will resurface at some point to taunt me and to insist on reconsideration. I may sit and read, write, teach, talk, and still an important point will come to me when I am far from a pen and paper and my (conscious) mind is elsewhere.

Psychoanalysis turns rationalist stories about thinking on their head: the thoughts come first and thinking (may) follow. Thought, thinking and affect are inextricably bound together and anchored fast in the unconscious – a place we cannot follow. Bion states the case most clearly when he asserts that 'thinking has to be called into existence to cope with thoughts' (1967: 111). Where does this assertion come from, and what implications does it have for learning and teaching?

What does it mean to think and to know?

To begin to make sense of psychoanalytic stories of thought and thinking it is necessary to travel back to Freud in order to move forwards. As de Sautoy found, much thinking seems to happen in the unconscious and so it is to the unconscious, and especially unconscious anxiety, that we turn to seek out thought. In his later work 'Inhibitions, symptoms and anxiety' (1926), Freud conceived of anxiety as the source of repression and hence the root of the unconscious. He suggested that there are two closely related sources of anxiety: trauma and danger. Frosh explains that anxiety from trauma is evoked when the ego is faced with tensions it cannot manage; this would include all 'situations of extreme non-satisfaction' (1999: 65). He goes on to explain that in situations where anxiety is provoked by a perception of danger, the danger is 'usually concerned with losses or separations, because it is these which might place the individual in a position in which she or he experiences unsatisfiable desire' (Frosh, 1999: 65). In this situation, as he points out, the anxiety from danger circles around and becomes traumatic. In this way, anxiety becomes unavoidable and with it come the inevitable defences against anxiety (repression, splitting, projection and so forth).

The notion that the unconscious is structured around anxiety and that our lives are shaped by responses to the demands of the unconscious is unsettling. And this is the unsettling fact that Klein starts with: Freud's recognition that, 'while anxiety is a threat which emanates from outside of the ego, it is also experienced as an internal and instinctual threat by the psyche' (Stonebridge, 1998: 196).

Kleinian object relations

> I have often expressed my view that object relations exist from the beginning of life, the first object being the mother's breast which to the child becomes split into a good (gratifying) and bad (frustrating) breast; this splitting results in a severance of love and hate. I have further suggested that the relation to the first object implies its introjection and projection, and thus from the beginning object relations are moulded by an interaction between introjection and projection, between internal and external objects and situations.
>
> (Klein, 1946: 176–77)

The newly born baby has no sense of itself as whole, no words with which to think about its 'self' or its body, no way to differentiate its body from its mother's or from the world beyond. It lives in a world of sensation and phantasy; that is to say it creates wordless images and thoughts to make sense of the senses that assail it. The very wordlessness of our first experiences makes them impossible to think about; we need to symbolise our experiences (assign images or sounds) to think them.

The similes we use once we have entered language give us some idea of the terrors of these first experiences: *gnawing* hunger makes our stomachs *growl*, loud noises *split our ears* and leave our heads *ringing*, we fear that stress will cause us to *crack up* or *fall apart*. With no words to describe these phantastic assailants psycho-analysis labels them 'objects' – objects are aspects of life that we come to relate to. They may be internal or external (the baby and the unconscious have no way to dif-ferentiate), they may relate to parts of bodies that will later seem bizarre but which, in the beginning, are experienced as terribly real:

> [T]he child's earliest reality is wholly phantastic; he is surrounded by objects of anxiety, and in this respect excrement, organs, objects, things animate and inanimate are to begin with equivalent to one another. As the ego develops, a true relation to reality is gradually established out of this unreal reality.
>
> (Klein, 1930: 98)

These experiences of fragmentation, of living in a swirl of good and bad objects and part-objects, are labelled as schizoid.

Let us begin with the experience of hunger (for example). A growl from the stomach initiates a gnawing pain – some malevolent object has set up a chain of experiences which threaten to annihilate the baby's fragile existence: pain, loud noises in the ears tear the head, tears in the eyes blur vision, dryness in the throat scratches and generates more noise, mucus fills the nose and throat adding to the difficulties of breathing. Screaming to escape the screaming that fills its head and saturates its world with terror, the baby is 'beside itself' with rage and misery. The pain is experienced as malevolent, death-dealing, terrifying. To manage the pain an object is phantasised, imagined into being, an object that has caused this pain and to which the baby can turn its fury,[1] a malevolent object that Klein called the bad breast.

Of course, the world of the baby is not only one of pain and unexpected and unpleasant experiences. There is also the delight of feeding, of feeling warm and dry, of 'sustaining' arms and the heavenly bliss of safety, satiation and sleep. There are feelings of fullness, of 'no-pain', of security, there are gentle sounds that delight the ears, sights that gladden the eye; our cup 'runneth over' and we are filled with glory and gratitude. To keep these delightful experiences safe from the anxi-ety aroused by the dreadful ones, a new object is conjured. The good object, the good breast, brings life, hope and love.

It can perhaps now be imagined that the baby comes to feel persecuted by the bad breast – the growl comes to taunt and torment. As Freud suggested, the trau-matic situation (of helplessness and extreme non-satisfaction) has been joined by one in which there is danger. Klein's work led her to suggest two sources of dan-ger: 'the subject's own sadism, and the object which is attacked' (1930: 97). Anxious and furious, the baby seeks to destroy this monster, tearing, biting, kick-ing – but, just as it metes out destruction a new terror grows: perhaps the monster will bite back. To pile on the anxiety, the good object might perhaps begin to resist and stop giving, perhaps the infant's greed will generate rejection – another terrifying prospect. If the good breast is lost there will only be the frustrating bad breast. Here is a paradox, the objects now have a phantastic existence separate from the sensations that conjured them. They also have agency: they may want revenge, either for the hurt or for the greed; they bring danger. There now exists a state of paranoia.

The state and process of splitting and the accompanying anxieties are what Kleinians term the paranoid-schizoid position. This is a term whose proximity to labels of madness can frighten and cause some to reject it, yet it describes a way of imagining the beginnings of thought. Here is the first answer to the questions: 'How do we come to live life in the world?' and 'How do we learn?' The suggestion that we learn through overcoming the defences of the paranoid-schizoid position is not a comfortable answer.

In splitting its anxious experiences into absolutes of life and death, love and hate and phantasising these as residing in good and bad objects, the child has conjured up objects with which to defend its fragile ego. Life and death are not within it, they now reside elsewhere. In Kleinian language, the anxious experiences have been split and projected elsewhere. Feelings and experiences projected elsewhere may be left 'out there' or they may be taken back, introjected. As the good breast comes to be experienced as 'mine', so a positive sense of self and some resilience can begin to develop. As the bad breast is introjected, so the superego can emerge to censor phantasy and action. A process we come to call 'thinking' has begun, and it is wordless and resides in the unconscious. Aspects of thinking will always reside in the unconscious, especially in dreaming and that state of dreaming we enter when awake that psychoanalysis calls reverie; an apparently vacant state of daydreaming such as de Sautoy experienced on his fateful train journey.

So a difficult experience is split and the bad aspect is feared and subjected to what Klein terms sadistic attacks. The splitting results in feelings of persecution: the bad breast persecutes the infant by not supplying what is needed; further, it may be experienced as delighting in withholding its goodness: no wonder the baby gets furious! It has to be borne in mind not only that this complex story of love and hate, gratification and frustration, is phantasised (and therefore unconscious), but also that the breast is neither good nor bad. As Alford reminds us, 'the world is not divided into black and white; only our primitive mental processes are' (1998: 123). 'Good' and 'bad' breasts are entirely the baby's creation; they are projections of the infant's own feelings of gratification and frustration, love and hate. The child's own extreme sensations are intolerable and so, to survive them, they are split off, projected and phantasised (dreamed, imagined and created) elsewhere.

The absolute splitting of good and bad, nurturance and poisoning, satisfaction and frustration is a defining characteristic of the paranoid-schizoid position. Here, in a paranoid move, the hated breast (the thing that I cannot bear) becomes the hating breast (a thing that hates and cannot bear me). Simultaneously, the good breast is idealised as a saviour and, while the bad can be expelled (as a 'shit idea' for example), the good might be taken in, introjected and perhaps coveted.

Developmentally, as the infant comes to perceive the whole person and to see that the good and bad exist together in the same person, the paranoia evoked by its furious attacks is transformed into guilt. Juliet Mitchell (1998) explains that, rather than fearing retaliation, the baby comes to feel 'guilt and anxiety for the damage it itself has done in phantasy'. This Klein calls the depressive position:

> In overcoming this position the baby wishes to undo or repair the earlier phantasised destruction of the actual and the internalised mother. As it does so it also takes in the actual and the damaged and then restored mother, adding these new internalisations as part of the self's inner world. These two positions, the paranoid-schizoid and the depressive, develop in the first months of life, but they always remain part of our personality, of our normal and our psychotic development.
>
> (Mitchell, 1998: 20)

So what is good and what is repaired are introjected, taken in, and become available to enable (perhaps) the management and processing of further anxieties and splits. 'If,' as Hinshelwood says, 'the good internal object is felt to be possessed for all time ... it gives strong support and confidence when the subject is under stress' (1994: 79). In the depressive position, fear and hate are balanced by love and concern; the absolute splitting of good and bad is replaced by ambivalence. Ambivalence and the depressive position signal 'an increased understanding of psychic reality and a better perception of the external world, as well as ... a greater synthesis between inner and outer situations' (Klein, 1946: 189).

When ambivalence can be tolerated, love *and* remorse, hate *and* guilt can be allowed to coexist and be experienced in relation to the same object. But, beyond the first few weeks of life, neither state dominates every aspect of psychic life: in different contexts and at different times we oscillate between degrees of paranoid-schizoid reacting and depressive thinking. It is to signal the continuation of what are often called 'infantile defences' that Klein called these phenomena the paranoid-schizoid and defensive *positions* – rather than stages. 'Stages' suggest the possibility of development beyond; 'position', on the other hand, suggests places to stand, to move from and return to but never lost or entirely overcome.

Little Dick starting to think

Klein's analysis of Dick, a four-year-old boy who was brought to her for analysis, is central to her understanding of the development of symbolisation and the ego.[2] Her writing about this analysis in 'The importance of symbol formation in the development of the ego' helps us to gain a sense of these processes in action and demonstrates how through coming to care anxiety and thought are liberated and mobilised so that thinking and learning can take place.

Dick and his home life are described in stark terms:

[Dick was] a four-year-old boy who, as regards the poverty of his vocabulary and his intellectual attainments, was on the level of a child of about fifteen or eighteen months. Adaptation to reality and emotional relations to his environment were almost entirely lacking. [He] was largely devoid of affects, and he was indifferent to the presence or absence of his mother and nurse. From the very beginning he had only rarely displayed anxiety, and that in an abnormally small degree . . . Undoubtedly his development was affected by the fact that, though he had every care, no real love was lavished on him . . . Dick grew up in an environment unusually poor in love.

(Klein, 1930: 98–100)

Klein goes to great pains to convey the extreme extent to which Dick was uninterested in toys, people, movements and language. He was clumsy and mostly spoke indistinctly. The extent to which Dick had failed to symbolise was, she explained, remarkable. 'In Dick symbolism had not developed. This was partly due to the lack of affective relation to the things around him, to which he was almost entirely indifferent' (Klein, 1930: 102).

Dick simply did not care about anything or anyone. In not allowing himself to experience anxiety he could make no connections, there was no access to the fragments he might otherwise allow to join. Specifically, in not experiencing and giving vent to his sadistic furies against the frustrating breast, he was unable to come to a sense of guilt. There was no work of reparation to do, nothing to symbolise, nothing to think. It was as if he lived in a vast empty silence, a dead void.

Through play and an encouragement to act out what little he did experience, Klein enabled Dick to begin to encounter his rage and his sadism (in the course of his play he attacked objects, damaging and breaking furniture and toys). During one play session, Dick

was seized with anxiety, and for the first time called me to him. Apprehension was now evident in the way in which he repeatedly asked for his nurse, and, when the hour was over, he greeted her with unusual delight. We see that simultaneously with the appearance of anxiety there had emerged a sense of dependence, first on me and then on the nurse, and at the same time he had begun to be interested in the words I used to soothe him and, contrary to his usual behaviour, had repeated and remembered them.

(Klein, 1930: 103)

She describes his progress and in this description, we can see a process of learning being enacted:

Every advance was followed by the releasing of fresh quantities of anxiety and led to his turning away to some extent from the things with which he had already established an affective relation and which had therefore become objects of anxiety. As he turned from these he turned towards new objects, and his aggressive and epistemophilic impulses were directed to these new affective relations in their turn.

(Klein, 1930: 105)

As something is learned so it becomes something new to feel anxious about but it also allows the learner to turn to new things or new aspects of the thing known to learn more about. Here is long division: I have some understanding, but my knowledge is incomplete, fragile, insecure, it may let me down. However, if I can tolerate all that anxiety, I can now work on this corner of my difficulty in a different way and so that I can come to know it better.

To make more sense of this process it is useful to turn to the work of Wilfred Bion who, after his early work on groups, went into analysis with Klein and later developed her thinking in particular ways.

Bion's theory of thought and thinking

Central to Bion's understanding of thought and thinking is his suggestion that the thought comes first and thinking develops to process the thoughts. This reverses the usual, rationalist story of thinking conjuring thoughts but it emerges from his understanding of Klein. For Bion, the oscillation between the paranoid-schizoid and depressive positions (which he signalled by the symbol PS ←→D) demonstrates the development of thinking, a move from 'formless chaos to coherence' (Symington and Symington, 1996: 80) as thoughts condense out of the fragmented snowstorm of unconscious part-objects and the traces of sensed experiences. If a thought occurs that cannot be tolerated it will be rejected and expelled (the paranoid-schizoid position) but, if it can be tolerated, then there can be a move to the depressive position – a move which *is* thinking. This can be a difficult and counter-intuitive formulation, but Klein's descriptions of Dick's learning (earlier) give us some access to what it might mean.

For ambivalence to be accepted an emotional experience that was once too dreadful to be borne needs to be tolerated. Whatever it was that once caused an experience to be split into good and bad needs now to be perceived as not so terrifying. What causes this new level of tolerance for a particular anxiety-provoking context is unclear, or rather, multi-faceted. Symbolisation will be part of the picture, reality-testing will also be important, resilience another part, thinking and the work of thinking yet another. Whatever happens, it was the emotional response that was once unbearable and had to be defended against that now has to be accepted: all thinking and knowing have their genesis in emotional responses. The emotional responses do not come second, they come first. For psychoanalysis, affectless, emotionless thought is an impossibility, a rationalist dream.

Bion calls the emotions that connect part-objects 'links', and he recognises three links: Love, Hate and Knowledge (L, H, K). The links hold together fragments of paranoid-schizoid experience generating a move to the depressive position and thought. We might think of the links as flavours of ambivalence. If the link is absent (−L, −H, −K) then what exists is not the 'opposite' but the absence. If Love is absent, what is present is not Hate, it is 'no-love' (−L), indifference. In this situation, some block has been erected so that (for example) the Love that should unite some fragmented elements cannot be experienced and they remain apart. In remaining apart they cannot be symbolised, thought about or known; no learning can take place. Ambivalence broken returns us to the extreme polarised reacting of the paranoid-schizoid position, it does not generate a new connection. But this state of broken links, the loss of ambivalence, is not 'nothing', it signals the return of the persecuting part-objects (or absences of parts). Frustratingly, links are tenuous. We may manage to tolerate an old anxiety more or less well for a while but thoughts will fragment again. Holding together the bliss and the fury, the love and the hate we feel for someone we are intimately committed to can be hard work, and we can, from time to time, fail and forget to think properly about them.

The growth of thought and (the failure of) symbolisation

For Kleinians, there is always a possibility that sensations, ideas, desires might be experienced as so dangerous and overwhelming that they are eliminated, projected out of the self and placed elsewhere. Symbolisation – naming, imaging – is a process that can take the sense of peril engendered by 'not knowing' and tame it.

> This conversion process – from sensations to experiences – contrasts with other processes of immediate discharge (evacuation) of feelings. For instance: hunger will be experienced in the tummy as 'hunger pains', say, and could be merely discharged as bodily pain to be treated with medicines, or simply screaming for help. Or those feelings could be held in mind and recognised as a condition which requires food – that is, represented mentally as hunger – to which appropriate thinking could then be applied, resulting perhaps in making a sandwich.
>
> (Hinshelwood, 1994: 173)

The pressure of the pain, the discomfort, the anxiety, the fear, has to be tolerated (not evacuated), to be thought about:

> If the capacity for toleration of frustration is sufficient the 'no-breast' [hunger] inside becomes a thought and an apparatus for 'thinking' it develops … A capacity for tolerating frustration thus enables the psyche to develop

thought as a means by which the frustration that is tolerated is itself made more tolerable.

(Bion, 1967: 112)

Symbolisation and thought can form a virtuous cycle (a continuous oscillation between PS ← →D). This is the cycle that would enable us to learn from experience. Not tolerating the sense of difficulty, the pain, the frustration, is always an (unconscious) option and some 'environmental failure' can lead to a failure in symbolisation – a failure to think and to learn – and a negative cycle, a refusal to learn from experience, can ensue:

> [A]ll thoughts are treated as if they were bad internal objects; the appropriate machinery is felt to be, not an apparatus for thinking the thoughts, but an apparatus for ridding the psyche of accumulations of bad internal objects. The crux lies in the decision between modification or evasion of frustration
> . . .
>
> Inability to tolerate frustration can obstruct the development of a capacity to think, though a capacity to think would diminish the sense of frustration intrinsic to appreciation of the gap between a wish and its fulfilment.

(Bion, 1967: 112–13)

For Bion a sensation, an expectation, an 'empty thought', can meet with the thing it is waiting for (its realisation), with an accompanying feeling of satisfaction. His example is that of the baby's expectation of a breast – something that will arrive to take away this painful hunger – and the 'good breast' might indeed arrive as soon as the desire for it is experienced. In this situation, in this immediate satisfaction of the need, a conception forms, the idea of the breast. However, where satisfaction is immediate no thinking is required, there is only the experience of pleasant satiation, of something known. A 'thought', Bion suggests, is specifically 'the mating of a preconception with a frustration' (1967: 111). The experience of not having the breast turn up at precisely the moment it is wanted generates a frustration, a thought. If frustration can be tolerated (rather than evaded) then the 'thought' can be the thing that generates thinking. And *this* thought may, eventually, meet with its realisation and become a conception – something known. That is, if the thought can meet its realisation, if it can be brought together with the thing it is expecting, then a conception can be formed: eureka! And Marcus de Sautoy can move forward in his work.

For this reason, thinking and learning are inevitably and constitutively difficult; psychoanalytically, thinking and learning are tied to difficult feelings and frustrations. There is no magical way out of this bind: it is part of the human condition. It is only through repeated experiences of surviving the frustrations and difficulty of learning that our resilience to the difficult feelings can be built. When we can test reality, if we are able to experience and observe our own survival in the face of expected annihilation, then the situation *might* be less terrifying the next time. But such self-learning is never uni-directional or linear, never predictable; reverses and losses are to be expected. Our difficulties and resistances to thinking and learning are unconscious; what will trip us into an inability to tolerate something is hard to catch and harder to learn. It is generally so much easier to evacuate the 'shit ideas' and do something less torturous instead.

At the stage where the conceptions or thoughts are still unnamed, they are, Bion suggests, flexible and their potential is limitless. At the point at which they become named, those aspects which do not fit the name return to the unthought-realms, available for other bindings – they are split off from the concept and return to the other, scattered unthoughts. The paranoid-schizoid ← → depressive cycle restarts elsewhere. At each stage, when a concept is refined, as our understandings develop, ideas that had been linked become unhitched and the parts of the origi-nal conception that no longer fit fall away. Forgotten ideas return to the unthought-realm but may come back to us at some later date, in some other con-text to demand our attention again. Our potential to go on learning and develop-ing is as great as our ability to tolerate returning to states of new not-knowingness and our ability not to foreclose our ignorance.

Putting this into an educational context

If the toleration of the emotional content of experiences is key to thought, think-ing, learning and coming to know, are there traces of these processes in the data? What traces might struggles with the unconscious leave on the lived experiences and the psychic life of the classroom?

'But I don't get it Miss!'

There are many ways in which a bad breast and its anxieties can be evoked in the classroom; the complaint that 'I don't get it' is one manifestation of this. Typically, if a teacher asks 'What is it you don't get?', in response they will get a blank look or an unhelpful 'IT!'; the missing thing cannot be named. On one level this is not sur-prising. How can we know what it is we don't know? But that response is too easy; knowledge generally fits into a web or mesh of other ideas and experiences. Something should be articulable, even if only with difficulty and support. When we enter an experience characterised by extreme states or certitude – whether of an arrogant, omnipotent state of knowing everything with great certainty or of a despairing state of knowing nothing with equal certainty – alarm bells need to ring; something is being defended against. The question is: Is there any possibility of thinking about who is defending and against what?

The 'it' that has not been 'got' suggests knowledge that can be considered in dis-crete packages – split off and separate from other knowledge. Discrete knowledge is one of education's sustaining fantasies. If 'it' exists then a good teacher could/

should/would give 'it' to me. The feeding/love/generosity could/should/would be 'natural' (if I were worthy of its receipt). This metaphor creates a mind that can receive it, somewhere to deposit the discrete knowledge-packages. Kleinian psychoanalysis rejects this metaphor. The mind is not a container, it is activity (Bion, 1967).

'Getting it', making understanding, comes from tolerating the anxious feelings of not knowing, of not being worthy of knowledge and teaching, of fears of a teacher's reproaches and peers' sneers. If frustrating anxieties can be tolerated then new connections might be forged between part objects that *already exist*. New ideas and experiences have to find their place, to settle in and join up. But, paradoxically, without some anxiety to displace into objects and things, there would also be no learning.

If 'I don't get it', then 'it' has been separated (split off) from its connection to what I do know, or a link between elements has been refused. As an example, take a common mathematical 'rule', one that is likely to be familiar. This rule suggests simply that, faced with the demand to divide fractions, 'you turn it upside-down and multiply'. The suggestion is that $\frac{3}{4} \div \frac{1}{2} = \frac{3}{4} \times \frac{2}{1}$ and the application of this rule is relatively easy. There is no imperative to understand what it means to divide by $\frac{1}{2}$, no need to forge links between $(3 \div 4) \div (1 \div 2)$ and $(3 \div 4) \times (2 \div 1)$ or $\frac{3}{4} / \frac{1}{2}$. No need to connect division by fractions with division by whole numbers. We do not need to generate a story about what is happening as we might faced with $34 \div 12$ (stories can suggest solutions). There is no need to connect all the other things one knows about multiplication and division to the strange action of dividing by a fraction. Nor is there a need to confront an answer larger than the initial quantity: how can that be if 'division makes smaller'? Leaping to an answer, especially someone else's answer ('turn it upside-down and multiply') before you have had time to even try to think – to try to forge your own connections – forecloses the possibility of recognising the other experiences which might have helped the operation make more sense.

Coming to know is an active process of tolerating anxieties and enabling links to be formed. Refusing to know is an active process of breaking links (splitting) and defending the self against seemingly impossible difficulties. Neither process is passive. Understanding one's options as a teacher in helping children face the difficult work of learning requires not foreclosing one's own processes of coming to know; it requires tolerating our own states of not knowing. We have to know that the hard work can pay off, that the dreadful monster that is 'division by a fraction' can be survived and that mathematics, while it persecutes us, also provides ways of thinking. There is a good mathematical breast in the mix too.

Good knowledge and bad knowledge

Education splits good and bad knowledge. The good curriculum must be learned and saved from the polluting effects of 'bad' irrelevant, non-curriculum material that devours time and clutters our minds. While the content of the curriculum is highly contested (see, for example, Ball, 1993), as 'stuff out there' it can feel relatively safe to engage with. Owning our own notions of what is worthy or unworthy of being known can give more trouble.

Understanding and learning to make use of the many conceptual models that are mathematically (or otherwise) useful is acknowledged to be a difficult business (Ma, 1999). However, not engaging with this difficulty would seem to be an ethical issue. During a year 5 mathematics lesson, Miss South seemed to be unaware that at least part of the difficulty the children were experiencing was caused because she was conflating two models of division: sharing and repeated subtraction. The question asked how many teams of five can be made in a class of 33 children. Phrased in this way the question needs to be modelled with repeated subtraction – taking away teams of five until no more can be made. However, in helping a child Miss South told them to draw the 33 children and asked, 'We need five teams – how are we going to do that?' This reversal of the syntax of the problem needs to be modelled with 'sharing'. While the two models provide the same answer, the modelling, the actions required to 'act out' the solution, are very different. Once the interchangeability has been understood, switching between the two can be useful, but until it has been understood swapping between them causes confusion: sharing (one for you, one for you, . . .) and taking away (here is a pile of five, here is another pile of five, . . .) are different actions. Having struggled to 'teach with meaning' and to contextualise division, she gave up and drilled the steps of the division dance. This is a common reaction to having to teach something we do not fully understand – and mathematics is replete with algorithms designed precisely to reduce the thinking that needs to be done when repeated calculations need to be performed with economy and accuracy.[3]

In the face of anxiety generated by our own ignorance and the difficulty of coming to know, theory and practice, understanding and 'doing' can become disconnected. The performance of a calculation and (perhaps) getting the 'right answer' are allowed to overrule the need to think through apparent discontinuities in what we think we know. It is easier to banish the uncertainty than work through what 'should be easy maths' because children are learning it. The fact that we ask young children to get to grips with mathematics that is conceptually difficult is foreclosed by our relative age and experience.

After the lesson, Miss South talked to me and her teaching assistant, Mary. She explained that she hates teaching 'this method'; she 'can't see the point as it just confuses them' – although perhaps it also confused her. In a denial of what thinking is and of the magic that de Sautoy revelled in she complained: 'You spend ages going over and over it and it takes ages before it clicks and they can do it easily.'

In confirmation of Bion's suggestion that we hate having to learn from experience and prefer to arrive 'fully equipped', knowing magically and instinctively, she seemed to be wondering why the children (any of us) cannot manage to do it easily sooner. It is as if there is a wilful refusal to learn, a deliberate rejection of her teacherly generosity which she now wants to hold back and protect. Why do they (we) need all this time, all this experience, before we can know and understand? What a waste of time! This logic devalues the journey and the effort required for its completion, preferring to reach the destination without breaking a sweat – a state of mind that makes travel a complete nightmare!

Miss South's conversation with Mary continued with Mary contributing an anecdote about her daughter's experience of mathematics lessons in secondary school. Mary and Miss South were in agreement: maths is confusing, we may not know why we are doing what we have to do when we learn the subject and why should we have to? It is extremely likely that Miss South and Mary are unwittingly repeating a curtailment of thinking that they themselves were subject to as learners, and that the repetition of the rationale for their actions enables them to continue to defend against the difficult feelings evoked. It feels preferable to have the difficulty removed by an empathetic teacher, a guide who can tell us to jump 'unnecessary' steps, who can enable us to skirt the miring swamps and the distracting oases. Difficulties need to be minimised. However, this solution amounts to removing opportunities for symbolisation and for learning – making the process of learning paradoxically more difficult. But their conversation was like a comfort ritual. Its purpose was to confirm mutual difficulties with mathematics as 'natural', not to further understanding or develop ideas. It served as some kind of salve or balm.

Is Miss South a terrible teacher? She had, as was the practice in the school, downloaded a plan from a government website and supplemented it with work from a well-regarded published scheme. She had consulted the 'teacher's handbook' as well as the workbook for children. In doing all this, she had behaved conscientiously and had certainly undertaken more than many teachers do. However, she had not undertaken her own planning for the lesson on division. She had not asked herself *why* she was being asked to tell the children particular things, what it was that particular activities were designed to provoke, or how she might respond when those things *were* provoked. The government website and published schemes are all designed to lighten the planning burden that teaching places on teachers. But the burden being lifted is the need to think. And it is precisely the need to think that cannot be lifted. A helpful (if somewhat patronising) desire to rescue teachers (perhaps in part from their own experiences of having been left not fully understanding the maths) and to make their activities 'foolproof' leaves them at the mercy of stranded children and exposed to the dangers of looking like fools:

Tina: Maths is hard with Miss South but easy with Miss Ruby.
AH: What makes it harder with Miss South do you think?
Tina: Because she doesn't understand – that's why she goes on courses.

But is Miss South really an incompetent and thoughtless teacher? How can we reconcile the image from a difficult lesson with this comment, made during an interview where she is reflecting on the importance of talk in learning and the role that a 'plenary' is supposed to play in safeguarding time for this to happen in every lesson. She repeats the common beliefs that explaining your thinking to someone else forces you to get it straight in your own head and will also help to fix it into your memory:

> If you talk about what you have just done you are far more likely to remember it than if you just sort of do it and then jump up, leave your books behind and run out to play . . . having the opportunity to sit down, talk about it, share ideas and experiences of what they have done means that they are probably not only learning from each other, but probably cementing it in their own minds as to what they have done . . . I think it is probably very important for them to talk about what they have learned in a previous lesson, but I think what we don't talk about when we do a plenary is . . . we will talk about what we have done and what experiences we have had, and maybe if there are any questions that have come up, but we don't talk about whether it was a valid learning experience for them or whether they would have learned more if we had done something differently.

There is clear evidence here that, in an interview with someone from a university, Miss South can know that discussing the processes of learning is a valuable activity. Unfortunately, the pressures and stresses of an accountable classroom mean that there is not time: the luxury of reflection must be dispensed with. Such a response may also be a relief; facing a class of 30 children can be overwhelming – perhaps especially when one's own anxieties are precluding thought.

Creating space to think

There is a fear in education that the serious business of learning might be damaged by a lack of seriousness: so much to know, so little time to know it in. Play is banished to the playground, time is regulated, the teacher's authority jealously guarded. Endless exhortations to 'think about it' assume that thinking is a conscious, rational, deliberate action, that it can be sustained all the time and at full-power. Attention will not, must not, wander. These are assumptions this chapter has challenged. So where is the space to think? Some suggestions are explored here: play, collaboration and displacement.

Play and playfulness

While children often sought to respond playfully to teachers' questions, teachers rarely entertained children's imaginative (often indirect) responses. We never saw a fanciful suggestion used to refocus a lesson; in all our observations teachers stayed with their lesson plans closing down even potentially more productive lines of learning. This amounts to a foreclosure of an opportunity to think and to learn. Play and playfulness are 'inherently exciting and precarious', they 'imply trust' and, importantly, in play, anxiety (so long as it is not too extreme) can be tolerated and explored (Winnicott, 1971: 69–70). Playful situations provide opportunities for thoughts and ideas to be brought together in unexpected ways. The rich mix of dreamy associations mobilised by playful thought offers a forum where half-thoughts can meet their realisations, where 'frustrations' might be tolerated and thinking can take place. Far from being an enemy in the classroom, playfulness offers wide opportunities, if they can be grasped by a brave teacher who can tolerate not knowing where the wild thought will take them. There is always the option, if necessary, to redirect attention in the same spirit, without crushing the urge to engage lightly and with curiosity. It is such a shame that play is relegated to the nursery and playground. Finding space for it at secondary schools and in universities is even more difficult.

Collaboration and displacement

One characteristic of play is that, while it can be engaged with in isolation, it is often more fun (and more productive) with friends. Children were rarely given opportunities to collaborate, and we saw no evidence of their being supported to develop the skills required to enable collaboration to be productive. Opportunities to 'discuss' often degenerated into comparing answers or racing to see who could get the most done. But children were aware that there was a problem as the following extract from a group interview shows:

Yasmin: You just keep on writing and writing and writing and it's like 'am I bovered?'
AH: Does it matter what you're writing do you think?
Katie: Sometimes I'm getting nervous because I don't know what to write.
Fatima: Sometimes they say you have to write a story and you can't think of any ideas and when the teacher comes near you it's like you're going to get in trouble.
AH: But you just can't think of anything?
Yasmin: No I had a feeling that I just couldn't think and everybody started writing and I was like 'I don't know what to write, I don't know what to write'.
Katie: And I'm looking at the clock waiting for playtime. [Laughter]
Yasmin: No, no after like 30 minutes it's like 'oh what am I gonna write?'
Fatima: Yeah, everybody else is writing except for me.
Katie: Everyone else is writing like apart from me and Yasmin, cos we like sit next to each other and we have to help each other and we don't know what to do.
Fatima: Meena used to sit near me but now she's gone so I have to sit with the boys.
AH: Yes, I've noticed that.

The difficulty of having to deliver creativity on demand was exacerbated by the difficulty of knowing how to help each other. This difficulty was further compounded by the difficulty of trusting that collaboration really was being encouraged (so often it was labelled 'cheating'). A sense of paranoia and envy pervades the comments: others can write, I can't; others have ideas, I don't; others can share, I can't – and all is about to be revealed as I have not written anything, which means I have not done anything and it is the doing that counts. This conjunction of responses generated huge anxiety and a sense of stuckness that was hard to move beyond – especially as it was never made the object of thought.

Not only was thinking about thinking not possible, but actions and activities that children (or any of us) might undertake while we *are* thinking were simultaneously condemned. The kinds of 'mindless' activities that allow us time to process or focus – absent-minded colouring, doodling, stroking, fiddling with pens, thumb-sucking (smoking, eating or gazing out of train windows) – were all discouraged and those who sought to engage in them condemned:

Beyoncé: Can I stick my pictures in my book?
Miss Warner: Beyoncé, you have a flibbidy-blibbit brain. You're thinking of everything else but the work.

That thinking might sometimes be best approached obliquely was not an idea that could be explored.

Conclusion

In his consideration of the hatred of learning from experience, Bion discusses the difficulty of knowing when an analytic group begins: 'After groups have assembled, but before they have become used to the technique,' he says, 'there is a pause while everyone "waits for the group to begin"' (1961: 88). This is also a problem familiar to the classroom: When does the lesson (or learning) begin? Do we tell children that learning starts when they enter the school gates? After the register has been taken? When the teacher starts talking? (Why do we insist on silence while the register is taken?) In the university, does learning take place in lectures, in seminars, or at home? What is the status of homework and preparatory reading? Are they preparation, consolidation or practice? Are these something different from learning? To what extent does thinking about when thinking or learning starts in schools conceal messages about where, when and if it stops?

A consideration of when the lesson starts reveals the splitting of opportunities for 'good' learning from opportunities for 'bad' no-learning or un-learning (forgetting). We tell ourselves that learning happens 'here and now' not 'there and then'; learning happens by listening to the teacher not listening to your friends. And learning can be taken as an object and split into 'good' and 'bad' learning. At its most obvious there are distinctions drawn between conceptual and rote (deep and surface) learning, between what is original and what is pastiche or plagiarised. Education's biggest and most potent distinction, though, would seem to be between 'good' knowledge and 'bad' ignorance. Not knowing is a deficit that has to be made good but can never be completely overcome. Of course, the two belong together but the ignorance, the not-known, haunts and persecutes us. The existence of ignorance is a shameful secret whose potency can be read in the stings of taunts: thicky, dullard, dolt, idiot, moron.

A difficult thought for education to bear is that thought and thinking are uncontrollable, radical and subversive. We cannot control another's thoughts. And the time of learning – the nine to three-thirty of the school day, the time of the seminar or the lecture – cannot contain the processes. This undermines the teacher's authority: it is a fundamental uncertainty at the heart of education. As Marcus de Sautoy found, sometimes gazing out of a window can be highly productive. But gazing out of the classroom window is often seen as a threat to the teacher's authority, and anyone caught doing the gazing is likely to be reprimanded. Time is being wasted; you are not thinking! Britzman remarks on the 'curious time of teaching': 'Teachers feel pressure to "cover the material", students feel pressured to learn quickly, and disciplinary structure supposes the possibility of discrete knowledge, a knowledge that can be learned in time' (Britzman, 1998: 54).

This remark, *a knowledge that can be learned in time*, playfully encompasses a wistfulness both that knowledge should be learnable in a predictable, linear, chronological framework, and that it can happen in a timely fashion – preferably before the examinations roll around. Such a fantasy acts to keep at bay the unpredictability of learning and the impossibility of containing and controlling thought and thinking. Time and play are the great enemies of schooling, yet time and play underpin creative thinking and learning. Kleinian theory undoes time and temporal development:

> The adult is never free of the infantile processes: there is no pure, rational, objective separation between epistemological and emotional life. Rather it is the infantile mechanisms that make all knowledge and judgement possible. What inhibits the acquisition of knowledge is also what makes the acquisition of knowledge possible.
>
> (Phillips and Stonebridge, 1998: 7)

Time and psychic space are needed for frustrations to be experienced and tolerated, for thought to seek (and find) its realisation, for communication to enable symbolisation, for the unthought to become thought, for connections to be made, for dreaming and reverie. But education knows no such time; it is a rational endeavour wedded to linear notions of time that flows from then to now and on to tomorrow. Education skims over the development of the child in a conscious effort to drive (and deny) the unconscious.

Knowing all this will never be comfortable, and the curriculum still needs to be taught in scientifically flowing, rational time; one response might be to 'sleep on it'. But perhaps having some different ways to think about thinking may, from time to time, enable the knower to step aside for a moment and to ponder, driftingly, as the train rattles through the landscape, why (for them) all this feels so darned difficult! And while, of course, the dream or the moment of reverie may enable the thought to emerge clearly into the daylight, it might equally lead to repression, to the splitting and sending of the fragments back to the unconscious for another day. But maybe, just maybe, it now feels more worthwhile to take the time to think about it?

8 But I think best with my friends

Thinking in relationships

In the last chapter, I explored thought and thinking in terms of personal, internal processes. By contrast, this chapter explores pedagogic and peer relationships as mechanisms for thought and thinking. The children in Grafton School set great store by their friendships and, as we have seen from time to time in the examples provided, experiences of isolation were difficult for them and were felt by them to interfere with their learning. At various times and with tremendous poignancy, children told us about how they sometimes struggled to work when, for whatever reason, they were separated from their friends.

Melanie Klein's theory of the paranoid-schizoid and depressive positions was looked at in the previous chapter. Coupled with the work of Wilfred Bion, the oscillations between the dichotomising paranoid-schizoid position and the more tempered ambivalence of the depressive position were used as metaphors to consider the way the psyche contains, manages and processes experiences. This model was used as a way to begin to think about thinking – particularly that aspect of thinking that is experienced as individual and personal; as going on 'inside my head'. For Klein, relating to objects is entirely an intra-psychic event. Her theory rests, like Freud's, on drives and instincts. The objects and part objects that are being related to are entirely phantastic, their persecutions reflections of inner anxieties, not external realities. Frosh draws a distinction between Klein who 'sees development as a struggle to live with ambivalence, to contain conflict and make something of it' and Winnicott, who 'assumes that development is "naturally" a creative, integrative process in which the infant's inbuilt propensities can be nurtured so that they flower into an integrated selfhood' (1999: 111).

This radical difference divides Kleinian psychoanalytic theory from object relations[1] and other intersubjective psychoanalytic theories. It is not that there are no continuities between the accounts, but rather, there is an optimism and externality suggested by intersubjectivity that is missing in Klein's work. In Kleinian accounts, the role of the actual mother is minimally important since the system is 'closed': things outside the self – other people and the social world – influence it but only in as much as they impinge upon it. However, 'for object relations theorists, the internal world is set into motion by sociality . . . and its structure and contents are the product of a collision between internal needs and real social forms' (Frosh, 1999: 116); it is social relations, rather than drives, that primarily generate the frustrations that fuel thought and thinking.

Jessica Benjamin has written about the connections between the Kleinian and intersubjective positions:

> The double action of intersubjectivity [involves] recognising the other's subjectivity and one's own ... the principle that informs [this] is the idea of transforming complementarities into dialectical tension, into tolerable paradox, instead of into antimonies that compel dangerous choices. Opposites are to some extent unavoidable because of the inherent psychic tendency to split; because, in fact, they allow the mind to think. It is the capacity to hold them in tension and overcome splitting that is at stake. The inevitable movement through opposites is what we need to hold in mind.
>
> (Benjamin, 1998: 24)

Containment and holding

What is at stake in an intersubjective account is the capacity of relationships to hold (tolerate/contain) tension (anxiety/frustration), rather than expelling it. Kleinian part-objects are *contained* by the individual's unconscious; for Winnicott and other relational psychotherapists it is the relationship itself that acts as a container. Initially this is inevitably the relationship with the mother:

> It is the mother's task to support the infant's ego after birth by falling into a state of 'primary maternal preoccupation' in which she has complete oneness with her baby and can provide her or him with perfect 'holding', allowing the child to gain a sense of trust in the world and security in her or himself.
>
> (Frosh, 1999: 109)

As noted in earlier chapters, a problem inherent in making the mother a more central figure in the development of the child's ego is that any difficulties the individual child may develop, particularly in relating and learning, might potentially be read as the mother's 'fault' – *she* must have done something wrong. The apparent 'naturalness' of this state of affairs fails to acknowledge that the maternal role is socially constructed and socially shaped. It also hides the child's real, separate existence. The romantic biologism of object relations can also be understood to carry an implication that the role of *mother* must override all other roles a woman may have at the time she gives birth. That is, the romantic dyad, the state of 'primary maternal preoccupation', must necessarily be a mother's first and only concern – a state that may not be possible or desirable, especially if, for example, the baby is not a first child, if the father or some other relative takes on the role of primary carer, or if either the child or the mother are less than well.

Despite all these difficulties, the work of Donald Winnicott and later intersubjective or relational psychoanalysts (see especially Jessica Benjamin, 1988, 1998, 2004) can be helpful when we think about teaching and pedagogic relationships. Chapter 4 detailed a Winnicottian vision of the newly born baby entering the social world. The account he provides, initially familiar from other psychoanalysts, is of a baby unable to distinguish itself from the world beyond; the me and the 'not me'. The mother, in a state of reverie in which she and the baby are *as one*, is able to process the baby's experiences and return them to him in a bearable form. She is able to 'hold' or 'contain' the baby's gesture (its cry or movement), experience its anguish and enable it to know that it will survive.

The psychoanalytic notion of 'containment' is important here in that it provides a metaphor for thinking about the work that relationships and minds might do. One difficulty, however, with using 'a container' as a metaphor is the enduring and static images that come from our everyday experiences with concrete containers which colour our imaginings. Whether, when we think of containers, we see images of delicate and intricately painted vases or of robust, utilitarian Tupperware lunch boxes, the containers of the material world have fixed capacities and rigid sides. Some are made of materials so fragile that care needs to be taken in their use lest they crumble or shatter (in fact it is probably safest to leave such containers unused on a shelf); others are so robust that we need give little thought to their use and can put them in hot ovens, icy freezers, dishwashers and children's school bags with relative confidence. Containers limit and define the shape of their contents. Further, material containers are passive, receiving their contents and holding them but not changing or being changed by that content. Herein lies the difficulty: when we think of psychic containers there is a danger that we may believe that what we need to be is some kind of emotional casserole dish – perhaps one with a well-fitting lid.

Psychoanalytically, containment refers to the reception of other people's projections or projective identifications (Frosh, 2002: 105). Our experiences with material containers let us down when we shift to considering psychic containers, and here again we can see the difficulties of thinking metaphorically. With the move from the material to the psychic comes fear. If I think of myself as a container: What if I am not strong enough and crack? What if I can't hold everything? What if I overflow and some of the contents are lost? What if I am the wrong shape, having rounded sides when the contents are square? What if the contents are caustic and corrosive – what will become of me then? Or perhaps I am caustic and will corrode the contents! And if I think of someone else containing me – can I trust that they are up to the job? It hardly bears thinking about.

These imagined fears are real enough; they shape the relationships we develop and the intimacies we can bear. Part of what allows the fear to take hold is the imagined passivity of the container, and yet containment, as a psychoanalytic concept, is very far from passive. We have all survived experiences of acting as containers for, and being contained by, others. And, in this relational, intersubjective psychoanalytic account, it is experiences of having been contained by others that have enabled (and continue to enable) us to grow intellectually and emotionally. The first experience of containment is in childhood. Winnicott's 'holding environment' offers an example of this (discussed in chapter 4): 'Striving to construct a core of meaningful selfhood, the small infant learns to trust in the reliability and responsiveness of the mother and hence, by extension, the external world' (Elliott, 2002: 69).

In adapting to the baby's needs and providing what is required to satisfy the demand of the cry, parents 'contain' the anxiety, hunger and terror of the child. And yet parents will tell you how hard it is sometimes to be a good parent – when the whinging, crying and dependency get too much, when the endless demands leave them exhausted and drained. And as teachers – at whatever level – we can experience individuals or groups of students in similar ways. As students split off or act out the emotional experiences that they cannot manage to deal with we can be left wondering how to cope – perhaps becoming anxious and overwhelmed ourselves. And these processes also operate in the other direction: from ourselves to our students. Yet containment and the existence of a task that can be embraced are at the heart of learning and knowing.

Jessica Benjamin and the intersubjective third

To make sense of relationships and the metaphors of intersubjectivity, it is useful to bear in mind Klein's paranoid-schizoid and depressive positions. I want to suggest the metaphors and processes in this chapter to some extent work in parallel with the oscillations between these positions. For example, while Klein's paranoid-schizoid position is an internal state creating extremes by splitting good from bad, Benjamin's doer/done to relationship is external and characterised by splits between what is possible/impossible within a relationship. Further, the thinking that was characterised as being a function of the move to the ambivalence of the depressive position finds a counterpart in Benjamin's 'intersubjective third'. These similarities and differences are developed further in what follows.

A third, intersubjective space between us

So what then is this 'third place'? In starting our lives in a dyadic relationship with our mothers (or other carers) we are in a place of unified twoness where the child is lost in the mother and the mother lost in the child. It is important in this fantasy that the mother presumes to know the child completely and the child presumes to possess the mother entirely. Here are two omnipotent forms of merger: one is a power-play (I am your mother, I know what is best for you), the other is devouring (I can take you into me and make you part of/the same as me); both deny the difference between 'me' and 'not me'.

There is a very real difficulty in learning and remembering that the other is not perfectly known, predictable and understood; too often the 'not me' is taken to be the same as, or equivalent to 'me'. However, Benjamin posits the possibility of developing relationships which she characterises as 'forming a "third space" of intersubjective recognition and experiencing. This third place is not entirely mine nor is it entirely yours; it is ours, it exists between us'.[2] The third space, she stresses, is always and only ever a place within a relationship; it is not some other place outside the relationship.

> To the degree that we ever manage to grasp two-way directionality [that in a relationship, I impact on you as much as you impact on me], we do so only from the place of the third, a vantage point outside the two. However, the intersubjective position that I refer to as thirdness consists of more than this vantage point of observation. [This can refer to] anything one holds in mind that creates another point of reference outside the dyad.
>
> (Benjamin, 2004: 7)

For Benjamin, our ability to co-create and surrender to thirdness is rooted in our earliest experiences with our mother (or other primary carer). Initially, there is the experience of having hungry anguish held, tolerated and relieved. The mother is able to hang onto the fact that the baby's distress will pass and, while she is able to recognise and empathise with its pain and frustration, she is not overwhelmed by it, nor does she run from it. She is able to 'hold the tension between the identificatory oneness and the observing function' (Benjamin, 2004: 14). In maintaining this tension, Benjamin suggests, the possibility of a third space can be created. The experience of give and take, of communication, first through gestures, looks and sounds, and later in words and sentences, provides a rhythmic movement which she suggests is also important in coming to experience and know the possibility of such a third space. The experience of back-and-forth plants the idea that my communications can be received and responded to: that I can be seen and recognised by you, and that I can see, hear and recognise you; it is in this space that hope and love are born.

For the teacher and learner in the classroom to develop this ability to create and surrender to a third space, the teacher would need to be able to hold the learners' tensions and anxieties knowing that they will pass. This teacher would be able to let the difficulty exist and facilitate the struggle, and would be able to let the learners know, at some level, that their struggles were okay, survivable and, with time and effort, surmountable. And she would be able to do this without becoming overwhelmed by the sense of difficulty or running away from it: giving an easier task, passing a child to a teaching assistant, resorting to schemes that mean specific planning does not need to be undertaken and so on.

A position of complementarity: you or me, doer or done to

In tolerating the child's (or learner's) discomfort, the mother (or teacher) processes its pain and frustration, thinks the thoughts, and returns them to the child/learner in a manageable form. However, if the mother/teacher is not able to hold the child in mind, if she overidentifies with the child, she may either swamp it (by *giving from a position of complementarity* in which she and the child are assumed to be one) – leaving it unable to learn to think its own thoughts, or abandon it – leaving it alone with the unmanageable feelings and similarly unable to process its thoughts/feelings:

> [I]f she gives from a position of pure complementarity (the one who knows, heals, remains in charge), the [learner] will feel that because of what the [teacher] has given him the [teacher] owns him . . . Further, the [learner] has nothing to give back, no impact or insight that will change the [teacher]. The [learner] will feel he must suppress his differences, spare the [teacher], partici- pate in pseudo-mutuality or react with envious defiance of the [teacher]'s power.
>
> (Benjamin, 2004: 14)

While 'a shared third is experienced as a cooperative endeavour' (Benjamin, 2004: 18), a position of complementarity in which one is active and the other pas- sive is characterised by a pattern of action/reaction and is one-directional, moving from 'doer' to 'done to', from the one in control to the controlled, from the mother to the baby, from the teacher to the learner. In this one-way exchange, the 'done to' feels invisible, impotent to influence his persecutor while the 'doer' remains aloof and apparently untouched by her actions. The plight of the perse- cuted does not impinge on the life or actions of the persecutor: 'If the [learner] does not feel safely taken into the [teacher's] mind, the observing position of the third is experienced as a barrier to getting in, leading to compliance, hopeless dejection, or hurt anger' (Benjamin, 2004: 28).

The mention of 'compliance' here connects with Winnicott's suggestion of the development of a compliant caretaker or 'false' self structure when the holding environment is not experienced as satisfactory. There is a psychic congruence between a holding environment, containment and being held in mind.

It is possible to recognise in the description of complementarity the teacher who would make things easier for the learner through an overidentification with her struggling pupils. Miss Middleton's 'I know, I found it hard, I couldn't do it either, push these counters together and re-count them then you'll have the answer' or 'As a teacher I would never do to children what was done to me in school' assumes the learner is reliving the teacher's early experiences. In presum- ing to save learners from what may not be their experience, the teacher abandons them to sort out their confusions alone. For the pupil caught in this gaze and over- protective containment there is no room to move or to think. From this position, maintaining the tension of holding the learner's discomfort while helping them process their experience is avoided; the tension is expelled in an act of identification. But while the teacher may feel relieved that the tension they experienced has been dispelled, the child is left with their difficult feelings of not understanding the work, and now also not understanding why the teacher has 'rescued' them (remember Muhi's confusion in his new maths group). Holding tension is never comfortable; helping a learner to understand why they are struggling and watching the painful process of learners developing understanding is much more difficult than solving the problem for them – but this is about the release of tension for the teacher, not the learning of the learner.

It is in maintaining a sense of sharing and collaborative endeavour and in managing to hold onto these tensions for each other that a space of thirdness is created. However, the development of systems of sharing and mutuality may be antithetical to the atmosphere in many of today's classrooms, dominated as they are by test results and the need to be doing better every day (Ball, 2003). The co-creation of processes that will be struggled for over time might feel too difficult, too demanding of time. Perhaps the process is even dangerous if your thoughts and movements are monitored through everything from your planning documents to the children's test results. In a climate in which the demand for control that permeates down from government to the classroom is extreme and unrelenting, letting go may feel impossible.

It is through the learner's engagement with a teacher they know and trust and who knows and trusts them that both can come to know about each other's passions (loves and hatreds). Further, it is through this interest in the teacher and their passionate engagement with the things we must learn that we learn the subject too (Bibby, 2009a):

Sally: The teachers make a big difference when it's subjects so I hardly have Miss Daniels ever but I had her once in maths and she wasn't the best. But when it comes to subjects I don't like but I have a teacher that I like then I would have a good standard. But if I had a teacher that I don't get along with, then I wouldn't get it.

In this comment, Sally seems to be saying something about the importance of the mutuality of a pedagogic relationship for 'getting it' – for developing the links that enable growth of thought (Bion, 1967). However, as we have already seen, holding the learner's anxieties and fear, tolerating their pain so that a place of intersubjective awareness (of thirdness) can form and be maintained, is not easy and can quickly founder.

Pedagogic relationships

Benjamin's suggestion that we might think of relationships in terms of the extent to which they can enable thinking and learning is an attractive one for educators. Elsewhere, I have used Benjamin's and Bion's ideas to ask what a learner-centred pedagogy might look like (Bibby, 2009a) and how particular kinds of pedagogic relationships restrict or facilitate the learner identities that are available to young people (Bibby, 2009b). Similarly, throughout this book there have been examples which could be reframed either in terms of a 'doer/done to' dynamic or (less often) in terms of the development and use of an intersubjective third in a peda- gogic relationship. In all the previous chapters, there have been examples of the different focus of the children and the teachers.

In considering the research data as a whole, we see that the children have strug- gled to answer questions which could typified as: 'Who am I?', 'Who are you?' and 'What is the difference between us?' Such questions move between the split char- acterised by 'me' and 'you', to the ambivalence of 'us'. The teachers, on the other hand, appear to have stayed stuck in a split state in their focus on: 'What level are you?', 'What level should you be?' and 'What do I need to do to up-level you?' The teachers' task seems to revolve around actively *doing something to* the learners. In the different stances implicit in these questions we might read the children's relative desire to establish two-way relationships and we might also gain some sense of the feelings of persecution they experienced as a result of the teachers' refusal to meet them anywhere other than on their (accountability-driven) terms.

Is this what democracy looks like?

Grafton School had a school's council and children were elected, on a yearly basis, to serve as class representatives. We did not get an opportunity to observe the council, and the class rarely spoke about it, so it was unclear to us whether the chil- dren felt much connection to it or its potential uses. We became aware of the coun- cil's presence towards the end of the children's time in year 5 when we saw the children at different times designing a new playground and a school uniform.

School uniform is an interesting topic arousing seemingly disproportionate passions in England. It was unclear how the issue of whether or not the school should adopt a uniform had arisen but it was clear that the matter had been put to the vote through the school council. Each child in the school had been given a vote and the decision was apparently taken on a 'first past the post' basis (the same way that UK general elections are decided). Mrs Norton, a teacher, mentioned the vote in an interview and was obviously pleased to be able to point to the school's inclu- sivity and democratic processes. Commenting on the feasibility of listening to the children's concerns she said:

Mrs Norton: I think their opinions are valid. What they think. What should happen next. I mean, they have school council in this school, where they express opinions to the council. It is nice to make them feel they are involved in something. But ultimately it is our decision, the teachers and the head teacher. But to make them feel involved and part of the school community . . . I think they do [feel listened to] because when we decided on a school uniform, for example, the children had a say in what colours they wanted, what kind of uniforms they would like. They voted on that. I think they felt they were heard and listened to.

AM: Did they want school uniform?

Mrs Norton: The majority of them did.

So this process was one of faux involvement. Somewhat patronisingly, actually, the decisions, the power, would remain with the adults; there would be no 'real' consultation. If the issue mattered sufficiently to the staff, the implication was that there would be no consultation (although there might be information) and there would be no vote. Mrs Norton seems to have felt this difficulty did not arise in this case since the children voted to have a uniform. But, we discovered later, the process had not been so simple. In fact the vote had no clear outcome.

How to deal with 'draws' in votes is an interesting topic which could have led to some generative statistical and historical research for the older children and some ethical discussions for younger children too. There are, after all, several models for democratic voting, each with advantages and disadvantages. In this case, rather than pass the matter back to the children, the parents were balloted and most of them wanted a uniform (the teachers will have been aware of this), so a uniform was instituted. This referral of the decision to the parents seems a strange action for a school keen to institute democratic processes. It is rather like deciding a hung parliament in London by referring the decision to a vote of the American population – not something that I imagine would go down well with many British voters!

It is interesting that the model of democracy implemented was so simplistic. There was no requirement for a particular percentage 'turn-out', nor a requirement that any 'winner' have a clear percentage advantage, as would be the case for trade union ballots for strike action, for example. Reducing the process to one of winners and losers, to what I want or what you want, seems a clear example of splitting. Reducing the conversation contained in the process we call democracy (admittedly, always a 'conversation' fraught with difficulties) seems a significant reduction of an important relationship to a one-way street. The other cannot be held in mind and thought about, there is no recognition of the need to build mechanisms for dealing with complexity and compromise, nor a discussion about why this might be problematic. Indeed, by passing the final word to the parents, the school seemed in the end even to refuse to take responsibility for their actions. Having responded to a popular move to 'listen to children' and instituted a school's council, it is worth reflecting on what one might learn in this pseudo-democratic environment – perhaps that voting and politics are not processes that are worth engaging with? But how was the (admittedly always problematic) relationship between an individual and the institution reflected elsewhere within Grafton School?

What kinds of talk are possible here?

Early in the spring term when the class were in year 5, during part of the time set aside for morning registration, the class engaged in an activity called 'speaking and listening'. We managed to observe this only once – it seems to have been a short-lived series of events that coincided with Miss South attending a course on debating. The field notes record Alice, the researcher's, expectations and experience:

> The day started with 'speaking and listening' which I had heard mentioned but never seen. I didn't really know what to expect but I imagined it would be something like circle time which involves responding to each other, listening to each other, etc. But what happened was, in pairs, members of the class had written a short piece of dialogue which they then stood up in front of the class and performed. Only two or three pairs did it this morning; others had already done theirs.
>
> They were surprisingly nervous standing up in front of each other in that way and there was heartfelt applause when they each completed their performance.
>
> While the applause was no doubt a genuine response, I had wanted to hear a kind of dialogue between the two standing up and the rest of the class about what they had written. There seems to be so little chance for them to share things with each other in the classroom and get feedback from each other, i.e. to speak and listen to each other in a real way rather than a performed way. I wonder what exactly they are being taught by doing this. What it doesn't seem to be is anything to do with communication *between* each other, it's more about communication *to* each other.
>
> (field notes)

In this extract, the researcher's desire for two-way communication stands in contrast to the teacher's insistence on communication as some sort of performance: as something *done to* the listener, not something to be actively engaged in by all parties. The final reflection hints at the maintenance, by the teacher, of one-way communication. An important question would be: Why might a teacher reject an opportunity for the children to engage with her and each other about their work?

The answer is not clear from the evidence here and perhaps it is not something we could ever be sure of; but we can think about it. The teacher may feel pressured by time and the need to contain the work in the time slot allocated to it (this would certainly be a familiar response to such a potentially open activity). She may be uncomfortable about the researcher's presence (although apparently there had been other, similar sessions, prior to this one). Perhaps she does not trust the children to discuss each other's contributions thoughtfully; perhaps she may have a fantasy about them becoming rude and having to regain control. Perhaps allowing the children free-rein might open floodgates that are felt to be better kept shut; she might have to deal with difficult messages to herself or between children, and that could be uncomfortable. Or perhaps there is some other reason. It is certainly possible that, in refusing their communications, the teacher is replaying some previous difficult relationship, that her reaction belongs elsewhere, perhaps in her own past.

The one-to-many nature of the exchanges in this example may have proved too challenging for this teacher in this context or at this moment. Previous chapters (especially 5 and 6) have explored the extra dimensions that groups add and these issues will undoubtedly have been at play here, for the children as well as for the teacher. So what about more intimate relationships?

On being a difficult character: Rezwana's experience

Evidence from the field notes about relationships with particular children is often very stark. One girl in the class, Rezwana, presented a difficult challenge for the teachers. This section explores the relationships she had when we first met her and throughout year 5. It should be noted that in year 6 her teacher arranged for her to meet with a learning mentor and her relationships in school began to improve. But the work began in difficult places.

Rezwana was a somewhat ungainly child; she was a little clumsy and slightly overweight but, to look at the class, she did not immediately stand out. However, the real and (apparently also) emotional poverty of her home life made her the target of some children's attentions – often unkind but sometimes tinged with pity. At various times children explained to me that her family did not have any money so, for example, she had to wear shoes that were too big, stuffing paper in the toes to make them fit. There were certainly difficult dynamics within the family. Rezwana's father assumed a very traditional, patriarchal role and, for example, became furious when his wife rearranged an appointment with a teacher to a time he couldn't make; by all accounts his opinion of women was not high.

Acutely self-conscious, Rezwana often spoke in a squeaky voice and mumbled, tipping her face to the floor. At one point in the staffroom I overheard her being likened to an 'Ewok' (a small, furry creature in a *Star Wars* film). Her peers also found her strange, although some were more tolerant of this than others. As Sharmily noted: 'Rezwana is the oddest girl in the class, and the oddest girl in the school . . . the oddest girl in the universe!' But Rezwana did not always act as a passive victim; she could also fly into a fury and was capable of shouting at children in the playground and standing up to (some) teachers. She seemed to have no real friends and often attached herself to one of the research team during playtime. In this extract from the field notes, the researcher, Alice, reflects on her experience of being around Rezwana:

I am very fond of Rezwana actually and notice that she is often the butt of teachers' jokes in the staffroom (especially Miss South and Miss Middleton).

It seems that they can't be bothered to try and understand her or at least understand why she has such trouble communicating. I tried to broach this with Miss South who told me that her father is very belittling of females and barely recognises her. Rezwana has often made overtures to me, more often than not in the vein of 'think of a number between 1 and 100' after which I have to multiply, divide, take away some number or another at the end of which she is able to say what my original number is. It can get a bit tedious but she's trying to engage. She has gradually begun talking to me more, and today in the playground at break we had a long chat. It was a perfectly normal conversation and she was speaking perfectly normally. As we walked together to line up to go back to class, Miss Middleton (who is often rude to her face) shouted to me, 'You can't leave, Alice, you're the only one who understands what she's saying!' I felt really cross, firstly because she said this not only in earshot of Rezwana, but in earshot of the whole class; and secondly because frankly she has never spent sufficient time with Rezwana to get beyond the squeaking; and thirdly because – rightly – Rezwana doesn't trust her because she is not kind to her.

(field notes)

Rezwana lacked the easy familiarity of some children but she was persistent and clearly wanted to form more mutual relationships. However, she did not experience the environment as safe: most people (adults and children) provoked and belittled her. To an outsider, it is clear that the ways in which she tried to test the safety of adults (and children) was counterproductive. Her opening gambits appeared strange but it seems that few bothered to wonder why Rezwana was finding it difficult to communicate or how they might enable her to get beyond her gaucheness. There was recognition that her home environment might not be conducive to developing a sense of self as likable, but no one thought that this might be impacting her life and relationships at school. As Alice found, a little patience and time to enable Rezwana to gain some trust was well rewarded.

During the research that the children undertook as part of the larger study, Rezwana in particular engaged with great seriousness, making efforts to keep a research journal. It seemed that for her there was a desire, a hope, that the research process might enable some reparative work to be undertaken. We were somewhat surprised when she decided that she would interview Mrs Norton – a teacher with whom she had a difficult relationship. Part of the interview is reproduced here; the tone of the extract is typical of the whole. The children had planned an aide memoire and practised asking questions and extending these with prompts. In the small research group Rezwana had been particularly good at this, the formal structure of an interview perhaps giving her a model for engaging with someone else. The terseness of this interview was a new (and disappointing) experience for her:

Rezwana: What is the most important thing you have ever learned?
Mrs Norton: Maths. It's true. Now which one?

Rezwana:	What is the least, huh? Oh yeah. What is the least important thing you have ever learned? Boring. [whispers]
Mrs Norton:	That's not very nice is it?
Rezwana:	I tried it on some other teachers and they had more interesting things to say.
Mrs Norton:	I can't understand what you're saying.
Rezwana:	Nothing. Read the question.
Mrs Norton:	What kind of sports do you like to play? I used to like to play hockey.

This is a difficult extract to make sense of but the exchange in the middle seems particularly revealing. There is a moment when Rezwana really lets Mrs Norton see what is happening for her: the responses are 'boring', Mrs Norton is disappointing Rezwana. Mrs Norton responds by saying she cannot understand what Rezwana is saying. While Rezwana's voice was very clear on the tape this comment may be a more general one. However, Rezwana gives up. She responds to Mrs Norton's treatment of the interview as a verbally administered questionnaire ('Now which one?') by telling her to read the questions for herself.

Benjamin suggests an impasse is created between the 'doer' and the 'done to' and that the relationship can be characterised by

> coercive dependence that draws each into the orbit of the other's escalating reactivity. Conflict cannot be processed, observed, held, mediated, or played with. Instead, it emerges at the procedural level as an unresolved opposition between us, even tit for tat.
>
> (Benjamin, 2004: 10)

In the exchange between Rezwana and Mrs Norton we see enacted this impasse, the tit-for-tat or a one-way, doer/done to relationship. We can well imagine both Rezwana's and Mrs Norton's feelings of annoyance and perception of not being understood, of being 'got at' (persecuted) by the other. From Mrs Norton's adult, teacherly point of view there may be suspicion about the interview and the motives of the researcher; she is, after all, 'only a child'. Perhaps, wanting to refuse the interview request but feeling unable to, she was rebelling against what she experienced as intrusion and compulsion; we do not know.[3] From Rezwana's point of view perhaps here is another adult not seeing her seriousness and her desire for a genuine exchange, another adult belittling her and dismissing her efforts. What is notable in this description is the lack of attempt (despite opportunities) to think about and try to take account of the other. While this might have been a big ask for both of them, Benjamin suggests that, until there is at least a willingness to try to do this, they will stay stuck in their unproductive relationship.

All the children's interviews with teachers were interesting. The extent to which a dialogue developed varied greatly and was affected by both the adult's willingness to engage and the child's ability to place on hold their nervous sense of not being 'allowed' to talk to teachers as 'normal people'. The interviews worked best where the adult seemed aware of the strangeness of the situation and was willing (and able) to reach out.

Frank: What games or sports do you like to play?
Mr Farrier: Football and tennis mostly. I like playing those. Although I haven't played, I play football a lot with my son. He's crazy about football. And my friend, Geoff, I play with him a lot.
Frank: What position do you play?
Mr Farrier: In football? Midfield. Keepie uppies.

The analysis of the interviews was undertaken by the group of interviewers (i.e. the pupils) together. It was a process they found very difficult but they combed the interviews very thoroughly and were highly sensitive to what they perceived as adults fobbing them off, to any lack of genuineness. They were dismayed, for example, to discover that the teachers *all* stated that they liked to eat out in their spare time and that they *all* liked teaching maths and English best and confined their dislikes to less high-stakes areas of the curriculum. They strongly suspected this was, at best, disingenuous, and were angry at what they interpreted as evidence of not having been taken seriously (or held in mind).

If it could only be like this: Rani's lament

It is difficult to find examples in the data of children being held in mind. Miss Warner's recognition of Rezwana's difficulties and securing for her the services of a learning mentor is one. It is notable though that the work of helping Rezwana develop her social skills was being given to a third person. Perhaps Miss Warner felt the time it would take her to do the work would be too onerous, or perhaps she worried that she did not have the skills. In a sense it does not matter. For Rezwana, there were now two adults helping her. Miss Warner was careful to keep her relationship with Rezwana constructive and positive. In this way, and through her acknowledgement of the work being undertaken with the mentor, she demonstrated that she was able to hold Rezwana 'in mind'.

Just before the end of the research I had an interview with Rani. Her interview, which took place in the classroom during playtime, was, in part, a reflective lament about the finding and loss of intimacy: about the process of the research, of her own learning through the research and throughout her time at primary school; about loss, growing up and moving on; and about fear and anxiety generated by the unknown, and particularly unknown relationships. In the extract that follows, we get some sense of the desired relationships. Rani is comparing the relatively intimate experience of being read to on the carpet with the more impersonal experience of being read to while sitting in assigned places at desks around the classroom and being expected to read along with the text projected onto the wall; the enjoyment of being read to and the work of having to listen *and* read:

Rani: yeah, yeah . . . On the projector it's like – when – I don't know – I don't – I do concentrate but I can't concentrate as much as sitting on the carpet and sitting with my friends and looking at it and talking about the story. [. . .] The carpet is really nice just sitting with our friends and listening and talking – saying our ideas. When we're talking on the chairs, um, the teachers think that we're talking about something else, about a different subject, but if we're on the carpet they know that we're talking about the story – like they can hear what we're talking about. [Now, my friends are] all on different tables and you have to talk like long distances and we're going to be distracting the whole class.

TB: So you can't do that [yeah] . . . so you're not as involved with things?

Rani: Yeah yeah – yeah, it's more boring in year 6 but when you're younger I suppose it's more exciting, I've realised that.

The intimacy and trust of the carpet, the physical proximity to the teacher who can interpret whispers, and to one's friends who can be touched or leaned into, the ability to exchange looks and gestures, is remembered fondly now that it is lost (the cramped discomfort of time spent on a grubby carpet, often waiting for the teacher to get organised seems to have been forgotten). The seating at desks, reminiscent of working postures and foreshadowing the secondary school experience, is colder, more distant; communication is in danger of being lost or misinterpreted. The carpet seems symbolically to have held the class in space in the way that Rani wanted the teacher to hold them in mind. The loss of the carpet seems symbolic of the loss of being held in mind. Of course, it was never that simple, but beneath the literal message lies a more poignant, symbolic one.

Conclusion

Benjamin's position

> defines intersubjectivity in terms of a relationship of mutual recognition – a relation in which each person experiences the other as a 'like subject', another mind which can be 'felt with', yet has a distinct, separate centre of feeling and perception.
>
> (Benjamin, 2004: 5)

For many this will be read as a romantic impossibility: we can never truly know the other, or indeed, ourselves.[4] The unconscious is unknowable and symbolisation (and communication) always miss some essence of the desire to communicate. These are serious points, yet there is, in Benjamin's position, something we can use as teachers to think about our pedagogic relationships. Unclouded and crystal-clear communication is not possible and we can never completely know the other, but we can work at making as little of a mess as possible; indeed, that would seem

to be an ethical responsibility. Communication is not transparent but we go on trying anyway. I can never know you completely but, if we work together, we may
each come to know the other a little better. Life is contextual and full of contin-
gency, extremes are unhelpful, difficult middle-paths need to be constantly
renegotiated and wobbled along.

The difficulty, and it is a very real difficulty, is in accepting that communication
is two-way and that the other is not perfectly known. Most relationships are characterised by a difficulty in acknowledging the other person as a separate centre,
someone whose subjectivity is separate from and different from one's own. This is
difficult because it requires us to recognise communication as a two-way street.
That means we need to accept, not only that someone may hear what we are saying, but that it will have effects on them that we can only begin to know if they help
us to understand them. We cannot safely assume we know the nature or the characteristics of a relationship without checking it out. To acknowledge the other, to
'hold them in mind', requires that we step beyond ourselves; as far as possible we
surrender our need for control so that we can 'see' and 'hear' what the other person is saying, not what we want to hear them saying. Benjamin characterises this as
a process of creating a 'third space' (not mine, not yours, but ours) in which both
can begin to experience each other's subjectivities and construct an intersubjective
relationship.

If this two-way street of intersubjectivity cannot be managed then we experience communication as a one-way street. In the one-way street of the 'doer/done
to' relationship, one party is experienced as requiring the other to submit to their
control. Ironically, the other feels exactly the same. An example of this, the way it
oscillates back and forth, its tit-for-tat nature and the apparent impossibility of
moving on, can be imagined if we think of Rezwana and Mrs Norton, or a 'difficult' class who leave their teacher feeling 'got at', invisible and deskilled. The
teacher feels persecuted ('done to') by the class while the class simultaneously feel
'done to' by the teacher who, by her nagging and shouting, appears not to like
them. Each experiences victimisation at the persecuting hands of the other; the
possibility of stepping aside from the conflict seems like an impossible fantasy.

It is unhelpful here to fall into the trap of constructing split notions of 'good'
and 'bad' relationships. However, exploring whether and how a relationship might
work to develop thought and thinking would be a useful task to undertake. The
demand for surrender of one's desire seems difficult – but surrendering what I
want to our mutual needs is not the same as submitting to your agenda. There is in
here a fine distinction that is worth bringing to reflections of classroom practice
as a way of beginning to hold the learner in mind. Sally explained the frustration
of submission:

Sally: It's boring, sometimes I write that on my book! And write graffiti and stuff,
          one time Tamara [researcher] saw me write it.
AH: And do you think it's boring? [yeah] Why is that, do you know?

Sally: Cos I know it and she just keeps going on about it. She doesn't get the point.

AH: Which point doesn't she get?

Sally: That I get it!

The difference between believing that children's (children in general and every particular child in every context) opinions matter and behaving accordingly, and saying this is what is believed but behaving in a contrary manner, is precisely what is at stake (see also, for example, Rudduck and Fielding, 2006). In an accountability culture, testing is used as an 'efficient' proxy for finding out what a child knows. The lack of engagement between a teacher and a learner while a test is being administered stands in stark contrast to the time needed to explore a child's understanding through working and discussing their work with them. Listening to children, to each other, is a very broad task which will not be managed all the time, but genuine effort can enable moments of 'us' to exist in the midst of the 'you' or 'me'.

9 Being 'good-enough' and taking the risk to 'fail better'

This final chapter aims to speak across the places of impossibility that have been revealed in the previous chapters: the unconscious anxieties and defences evoked by interactions between defended institutions, the defended self and defended others; the problem of identification and misrecognition in one-to-one communications and in the complex holding environment provided by the school; the difficulty of being in a group wanting both to belong and to be special; the dilemmas presented by basic assumption groups' responses to the need to work; and the ways in which mental states and relationships can act to facilitate or block thought, thinking and, ultimately, learning.

There is no instant solution offered to these 'problematics', but I want to explore the claim that I have made more than once: that teaching is a profession that makes strongly ethical demands. The particular demand I have in mind is the need to stick with the difficult necessity of walking a tightrope; a tightrope that might act as a link between easy dichotomies, the seductive splits between this and that, us and them, pass and fail, good and bad. I want to explore what it means to be forever in the process of balancing anxieties and realities in an endless effort to maximise ambivalence and thinking – even in the face of gales caused by policy shifts and turns, other people jumping up and down on the tightrope, and our own desire not to know. What does it mean to know that our defences make it inevitable that, however hard we try, our efforts will fail to some degree? Would it be possible and what might it mean to take as a motto Samuel Beckett's much quoted maxim: 'Ever tried. Ever failed. No matter. Try again. Fail again. Fail better.'[1]

The constitutive difficulties of living with our vulnerabilities and our dependence on others, our aggression, anger and hate, and the demands of our loves, needs and desires, all evoke anxieties and defences. Schools and pedagogic relationships are no more immune to these anxieties, frustrations and defences than any other institution or relationship. This book has drawn on a variety of psychoanalytic theories to consider some enduring difficulties associated with learning and teaching. While much of the original data came from one primary school classroom, I believe the message speaks to other educational contexts: learning is difficult whoever we are, whenever in our lives the need to learn is encountered and wherever it is undertaken. Fantasies of knowing and not knowing pervade all relationships although they are institutionalised in particular ways in schools; the pedagogic relationships of the primary classroom are not so different from the pedagogic relationships in other learning environments. The difficulty of keeping in mind both the metaphorical nature of psychoanalytic language and the strange timelessness of the unconscious and unconscious processes are problems of our defensive forgetting.

Throughout my explorations of psychoanalytic theories and classroom life, I have aimed to provide alternative ways of thinking about what happens when learners are faced with the necessity of learning and teachers are faced with the impossibility of teaching. In doing so, I would agree with many of the recent criticisms of therapeutic education. For example, that we cannot teach people to be happy, that insisting that learners 'confess' their vulnerabilities is intrusive and may be counter-productive, and that teachers have a job to teach, not to counsel (see, for example, Ecclestone and Hayes, 2009). Access to psychoanalytically informed supervision for teachers could be helpful – it is always helpful to have someone to help us think – but happiness is not something that can be taught, bought or bestowed, and policy directives suggesting that it might be are extremely problematic.

The attraction of a 'therapeutic' education, of an education that will cure the woes of the world, is undoubted. Therapeutic: 'of or relating to the treatment of a disease; curative' (Collins dictionary of the English language, 1986); so, an education that would treat the dis-ease of life, cure it. At the very least, if we could make sure that education today would inoculate us against ignorance tomorrow, if self-knowledge today could act to prevent disappointment and sorrow tomorrow, then the uncertainty and doubt that hovers out of sight, over the horizons of our lives might be less terrifying and perhaps we could be braver. We could be sure that we 'have the skills' to cope with whatever the future might demand and our dreadful vulnerability and dependence on others might be reduced. How reasonable is it to expect schools to perform this small service to society? After all, the terror is ours as well. In uncertain and fast-changing times schools earnestly develop individuals' study skills so that they will know how to learn once and for all; their dependence on us (and ours on other people) will be alleviated or removed. Imagine the financial savings to society . . . These hopes, while worthy and understandable, will inevitably fail. They are fantasies, wishes, dreams, so we remain perpetually disappointed when our students *still don't get it*, *still can't do it right*. No wonder the promise of a therapeutic education is so seductive.

The suggestion that Ecclestone and Hayes (2009) seem to take particular exception to is that we are all vulnerable and that the care of this vulnerability is someone else's responsibility. Indeed the notion that someone else can lift my vulnerability from me seems to assume the existence of someone immune from the psychic costs of caring to do the caring, perhaps somebody who has aged beyond vulnerability? From a psychoanalytic standpoint these suggestions are fantasies: institutional defences against the need to be with and learn from others.

One difficulty with 'criticism' in the classroom, school and other contexts is that it can invite splitting: I am right and you are wrong, tit-for-tat behaviours and the impossibility of thinking together. There is some evidence of this splitting both in policy and in Ecclestone and Hayes' (2009) rejection of therapeutic education. If someone else is going to assume my vulnerability, assign it to me, name it for me and presume to know how to 'cure' it, then we have a serious problem. I am likely either to collapse in a state of helplessness, or to explode with fury. Similarly, if my vulnerability is presumed to be a sign of weakness rather than a constitutive fact, then it will need to be defended against and denied: I had better pull my socks up and put on a brave face. However I respond to whichever dichotomised position, the possibility of thinking together, of creating some third space in which to consider the issue, is foreclosed; that the problem has been pre-defined and assigned or denied assures this – someone has been 'blamed' and someone else has to 'sort it out'.[2]

The pre-emptive identification of problems from the outside assumes that the experiences of the learner and the fantasies of the teacher are identical. Even if, from time to time, the pre-emption 'gets it right', the opportunity for thought and learning has been circumvented, an outcome that may not be right. The challenge lies in raising issues and enabling discussions in ways that can be engaged with; how can we invite entry into the difficult business of learning? Can we invite, or must we coerce or demand? What do we think it would mean for someone to accept an invitation to learn? What then would we expect of them?

Throughout this book, the difficulty of the assumption that we can know the other's mind and experiences has been pointed up in different ways. Whichever set of metaphors we use, we come back to Freud's insistence that empathy is problematic:

> We shall always tend to consider people's distress objectively – that is, to place ourselves, with our own wants and sensibilities, in *their* conditions, and then to examine what occasions we should find in them for experiencing happiness or unhappiness. This method of looking at things, which seems objective because it ignores the variations in subjective sensibility, is, of course, the most subjective possible, since it puts one's own mental states in the place of any others, unknown though they may be.
>
> (Freud, 1930: 89, emphasis in the original)

This is expressed differently by Benjamin who talks about the dangers of *giving from a position of complementarity* in which the mother and the child, the teacher and the learner, are assumed to be one (2004: 14). The problem is that when this happens, the person struggling to make sense of an experience is left unable to process their thoughts and feelings, robbed of a voice and unsure how to relate to the teacher who has overwhelmed them. As Muhi discovered when he was moved into a lower mathematics group, it can be profoundly unsettling to realise that the one who was expected to help has somehow compounded the problem.

So, what can a teacher do? Being encouraged to 'hold the student(s) in mind' might not feel very helpful when classrooms, lecture halls and staffrooms are permeated by the demands of accountability. Having one's attention drawn to less than perfect communication might evoke guilt, feelings of persecution, helplessness and anger. Such reactions come from a split place: a place hard to avoid when surrounded by policy imperatives to be a perfect teacher in an imperfect classroom, to ensure the class make the 'expected' progress when they fail to work as hard as they should (and whose expectations are these?), and to enable every learner to fulfil their (presumably boundless) potential when they resist teaching. It is not that teachers do not think, have not learned, fail to take their professional responsibilities and desires seriously. Rather, it is simply that thinking about these things is hard, and not to want to do so is an understandably easier option.

Thinking is not possible when one occupies a split, paranoid-schizoid position. But splitting is inevitable; our earliest terrors are evoked as we work with children and learners, and they summon memories of our own childhoods and the ghosts of learning-past. Thinking can emerge only when aspects of experience that have not been tolerated can be brought and held together. But a conscious desire for this to happen will not make it so. There are some splits that are riven into the education system at seemingly vast distances from the classroom, although their implications reverberate and impact all involved down to the youngest child in the smallest nursery furthest from seats of power. And to separate politicians from the impact of their policies is to forget that they too may have children and are part of society.

In 2009, Robin Alexander and his team published the findings of the extensive *Primary Review of Education*. The publication of the final report was widely covered in the media and welcomed by professionals working in and with primary education. However, the government's immediate response was to dismiss the six-year study as out of date and to reject all its findings (Coaker, 2009). This immediate closure of debates that the report might have initiated is not atypical of government responses to challenges to think again.[3] Educational commentators pursued policy makers' rejection of an invitation to discussion with increasing frustration.

When governments act as if they know what the problems and answers are, they leave teachers and others involved in education powerless to act, unable to engage them in dialogue. The very real difficulties faced by individual teachers and learners in particular classrooms are, under these acts of abandonment, unthinkable. Real people in real schools struggle to act in a context where there is little listening. It would be surprising if the lack of listening did not cascade down; no one is holding the tensions and anxieties. In rushing to act responsibly, no one takes responsibility; *caring about* has replaced *caring for*. At a very real and concrete level, difficulties within the education system are increasingly split off and located in 'failing schools' (Lucey and Reay, 2002). To protect 'good' schools, these 'bad' schools are split off from local control and expelled, as schools are moved from Local Authority to Academy control (see also Powell and Barber, 2006).

The price of perfection

Idealisation

Social fantasies about teachers are multiple but they are very similar to those of the perfect mother: a near telepathic ability to know their learners, super-organisational powers, creative ideas for engaging all children at all times and, above all, boundless love and self-sacrifice. Entering the teaching profession involves, at some level, a move to identify with these fantasies put on like coats found in 'the bric-à-brac of [a] props department' (Lacan cited in Frosh, 2002: 60). And like all fantasies, while being aware of them is one thing, expecting one's self to live up to them is something else altogether.

The experience of the impossibility of policy ideals and the sheer hard work of finding ways of living within them has been the focus of several studies (see, for example, Mahony and Hextall, 2003; Atkinson, 2004; Moore, 2006), all of which testify to the psychic and social costs that new identities levy. When symbolic representation – the descriptive labels we might want to attach to 'good' teaching – degenerates into 'symbolic equation', the role of the teacher becomes impossible and persecuting (see also chapter 2). In this kind of situation, a recognition that 'the idealised role of the teacher has failed' slides and becomes 'I have failed (to be an ideal teacher)' – a slippage in symbolisation that brings potentially heavy personal costs. To revisit some data that catch the trap of idealisation:

SC: Why do you think the teachers get so stressed?
Minnie: Because they want it to be perfect.
Rani: Yes, it all has to be perfect.
Minnie: They think we are perfect child, but we are not. We are just children.
Rani: Yeah, every child ain't perfect. There is always something . . .
Minnie: [Interrupts] Wrong with them.
Rani: Not wrong with them. But they ask that we all be perfect.

As Rani suggests, 'I cannot be the perfect learner my teacher wants me to be' is not the same as 'I am imperfect'. The slippage turns the 'problem' from one that resides within someone else's unreasonable expectations into a personal quality; from someone's idea to my identity. To what extent might it be possible not to comply with our own and other people's fantasies? Rational, conscious acceptance that we are not perfect and accepting the flaws and limitations of our actions is one thing; accepting our unconscious beliefs about ourselves is more difficult. What about the expectation that teachers, like mothers, must love their children? Where does this leave the unconscious and the non-rational?

Hate

Idealisation is a psychic defence: it focusses on the goodness of the good object enabling the repression of the bad: protestations of love ensure hate remains unthinkable. But, as Britzman reminds us: 'idealisation does not help the . . . teacher understand how the demands of the work affect the self who is working' (2009: 98). What space is there for 'the dark side of teaching' (Pajak, 1998)? Can it be seen at all? What can we learn from it? Why should we take the trouble? Britzman cites Winnicott who has one suggestion, recast here to address teachers rather than analysts: '[H]owever much [the teacher] loves his [students] he cannot avoid hating them and fearing them, and the better he knows this the less will hate and fear be the motives determining what he does to his [learners]' (cited in Britzman, 2009: 96).

The suggestion is that without knowing and thinking about the hate we bear our students we are in danger of taking it out on them; that, for example, our frustration at their repeated refusal to learn can lead us to behave punitively. Britzman goes on to elaborate on this warning, suggesting that 'unless the teacher can confront the defences of idealisation and omnipotence in her or his own teaching, there will be no real contact with others' (Britzman, 2009: 97). The issue of hate is difficult. How might we interpret it psychoanalytically? What might this hate look like? Drawing again on Winnicott, Britzman explains:

> [T]he mother must hate the baby without acting it out, her hate may be conveyed only through putting the baby to bed, lending the baby the terror of nursery rhymes and fairy tales of children being eaten or lost in the woods, and, eventually, sending the baby to school. But the baby, too, needs this hate because the baby 'needs hate to hate' . . . and also because the baby needs to know that it affects its mother. That is, in order to develop her own complexities and desires, the baby needs – as do our students and colleagues – to encounter a passionate, complex other.
>
> (Britzman, 2009: 99)

It is important that the mother, and the teacher, is a 'passionate, complex' other/'not me'. To be this, all aspects of the self need to be available. If, for example, hate or love are not present then the child cannot know the range of affects it generates in the other – it cannot fully know itself and cannot develop knowledge of its own affects and affective responses: it 'needs hate to hate'. If the mother is indifferent, if the love, hate or knowledge are not there, then the baby cannot know how it exists and it cannot learn to live fully – passionately – in the world.

In an interview, Miss South made strong protestations of love for the children in her class. Her comments began with her remembering the words of a lecturer from her training course:

She said – every single child in your class deserves a bit of you every day. And it really stuck to me . . . I adore my children in my class . . . the children are always in my head and I think about them quite a lot and dream about them from time to time as well.

Here, the goodness of her love is preserved and celebrated; self-sacrifice, the giving of a piece of yourself every day is a requirement, a moral injunction. What have they done to 'deserve' this piece of her? What happens if you give a piece of yourself every day? Does it grow back? Or do you end up feeling got at, pecked to pieces, depleted? How do teachers regrow the bits they have handed out? Is it wrong not to be so giving of ourselves? Is self-preservation unreasonable? Does her ownership of 'my children' and 'my class' mean she is giving herself to herself? Does this make the gift less threatening? Despite her conscious intentions, Miss South's actions in the classroom revealed that the situation was more complex:

This was a nice time to spend with the children as it was less structured. However Miss South spent the lesson firmly planted at her desk and asked me to supervise the group of girls who were sewing dresses onto their puppets.

(field notes)

Miss South was taking 'video' [an option during 'golden time', a reward time set aside during the week as payment for hard work] which is what she usually does, it means she doesn't have to interact with the children, help them, etc.

(field notes)

I asked [Miss South] why she wasn't going to be there this afternoon and she told me she had an application form to fill in. She is applying for the fast track to deputy headship, which she hopes to achieve in five years' time. Sometimes it feels that she is more interested in success or ambition than she is in the children.

(field notes)

The extreme love of the interview a defence against hate, and what emerges in the classroom might be read as indifference – a form of unavailability. A message of not caring, projected unconsciously, was picked up by the children; the apparent trust – of letting children get on alone – was counteracted by the indifference with which she seemed to abandon them. The boredom and lassitude that came over the class when this happened sometimes seemed like a reaction to the unthinkable hate: the 'waxing' of arms with sticky labels killed time – an action that is more acceptable than killing the teacher. What is it about children that teachers might hate? There are potentially many things. Their refusal to learn can be experienced as a rejection of the teacher's goodness and good feeding, the requirement of self-sacrifice which can leave the teacher feeling depleted, and their demand for caring and attention which evokes the teacher's own desire for feeding, care and attention: Who will feed and look after me? Who notices my exhaustion and despair? The classroom can be a lonely place.

What impact might a teacher's apparent carelessness or indifference have? Sally, reflecting on an incident from year 5, gives us an interesting insight:

Sally: Last year, when we did *The Tempest*, my head wasn't as good so then Miss
          South squashed my head.
Tina: [laughing] She what?
TB: It was a clay head wasn't it?
Sally: Yeah and she squashed it.
Tina: Oh right, not your real head . . .

In this extract, there is a telling Freudian slip or parapraxis – an occasion when, as the pun goes, 'you mean to say one thing but you say your mother'. Sally complains that Miss South squashed her head when she apparently meant to say that Miss South had squashed the clay model of a head she had made. The suggestion from psychoanalysis is that what she actually said is important – it reveals something about what her unconscious might like to say. Any interpretation of this is difficult as she is not available to test the interpretation with. Nevertheless, what might her opening statement mean? 'Last year, when we did *The Tempest*, my head wasn't as good so then Miss South squashed my head.'

This was a violent act. The literal destruction of the modelled head, the rejection of a personal and creative response to a task that had been given, will have been painful. The metaphorical experience of squashing, of having the juice (thoughts, creativity?) squeezed out of, or perhaps the life crushed from one's head is no less aggressive. Having one's head squashed might suggest many things. One could be that the head – the site of knowing and thinking, the symbol for one's place of worth in a school that focusses on knowing – is being deformed and destroyed. Perhaps Sally's head did not fit into the space that it was supposed to occupy and it had to be squashed in. Had it got too big? Had she dared to begin to believe she might know something? Had she become unacceptably confident in some moment? The tense and sequencing of the sentence is unclear: 'When we did *The Tempest*, my head wasn't as good.' As good as when? As it is now? Or as it had been before 'we did *The Tempest*'? Perhaps both? Does Sally feel she might have deserved to have her head squashed?

There may be other associations, and without access to the conversation we cannot be sure. Despite this, the calm, flat delivery of the statement suggested that Sally's own hatred of her teacher was lost in the moment. When she talked about the fact she was made to repeat the task, Sally confided that she did not do it; the energy required to recreate a 'better', more acceptable head was beyond her:

Sally: But, if you want to know a secret, Mary [the TA] did it for me again because
          I couldn't be bothered – Mary did it for me.

The inability to know the hate left her with no way to think about the experience. She seemed exhausted by the encounter and the effort not to know. Hate, like love and knowledge, is one of the links that Bion suggests can bring together affects and unthought fragments. These are the fragments – held apart in the paranoid-schizoid position – that could become thoughts if the frustration of their existence could be borne. And if they could be tolerated, thoughts, thinking and learning might follow. If hate cannot be tolerated, the hated object (affects, experiences) will be evacuated to preserve the loved object: in creating this split the unconscious defends itself against the necessity of thinking. In this way, banishing hate from the realms of experience forecloses one of the ways in which we can come to think and know. If hate cannot be known, what are we refusing to allow ourselves to learn? And how and where can aggression be displaced?

Aggression

Peter Maas Taubman uses examples from literature to explore hate in the 'caring' professions: a doctor in William Carlos William's *A Use of Force* (1937), and Ursula Brangwen who becomes a teacher in D. H. Lawrence's *The Rainbow* (1915). From the relative safety of literature we can observe how terrifying furies overtake and consume both professionals, and these furies seem shockingly familiar. The doctor explains his unreasoning pursuit of his own professional ends; his need to make well one whose illness endangers herself and, perhaps, others:

> The damned little brat must be protected from her own idiocy, one says to one's self at such times. Others must be protected against her. It is a social necessity. And all these things are true. But a blind fury, a feeling of adult shame, bred of a longing for muscular release are the operatives. One goes on to the end.
>
> (cited in Taubman, 2006: 24)

This self-serving justification for the use of force is extreme but still gets pressed into service to explain the (more symbolically) aggressive act of expelling a 'disruptive' or 'deviant' child from a class or school, or a 'failing' school from a Local Authority, to 'save' those who would/could learn and achieve.

The doctor, faced with a sick and terrified child, tries, with increasing frustration and escalating force, to open her mouth and observe her throat. When she had bitten through a small spoon, her father and a stronger spoon are used to 'win' the day:

> In a final unreasoning assault I overpowered the child's neck and jaws. I forced the heavy silver spoon to the back of her teeth and down her throat until she gagged. And there it was – both tonsils covered with membrane.
>
> (cited in Taubman, 2006: 24)

Similarly, confronted with a child who would not respond with gratitude to her narcissistic love and desire to 'save' him from poverty and ignorance, Ursula is overtaken with fury:

> Here [in this classroom] she would realise her dream of being the beloved teacher bringing light and joy to her children! . . .
>
> She would assert herself for mastery, be only teacher. She was set now. She was going to fight and subdue . . .
>
> So she snatched her cane from the desk, and brought it down on him. He was writhing and kicking. She saw his face beneath her, white, with eyes like the eyes of a fish, stony, yet full of hate and horrible fear. And she loathed him, the hideous writhing thing that was nearly too much for her. In horror lest he should overcome her, and yet at the heart quite calm, she brought down the cane again and again, whilst he struggled making inarticulate noises, and lunging vicious kicks at her . . . [A]t last . . . the cane broke him, he sank with a howling yell on the floor.
>
> (cited in Taubman, 2006: 25)

The terrible aggressive desire to do good, to cure, to rescue simultaneously strips the deserving, the ill, the uneducated of their humanity and the professional of the illusion of selfless care. The terrible price of their need to care at all costs is, Taubman suggests, the loss of a piece of their soul. In failing to confront their hatred of their patient/pupil, the hatred was, as suggested earlier, acted out on the bodies of those who they professed to care for and love. In these situations neither the doctor nor the teacher could gain any knowledge of those in their care.

Taubman turns to Lacan to explore what happens in the moment where the aggressive insistence on 'doing good' takes over. Drawing on religious stories of rescue and redemption and Lacan's notion of jouissance,[4] he explores two different manifestations of saintliness. There is a distinction, Taubman suggests, between the 'the good Samaritan or the saint who gives his own cloak to the naked beggar in the road' but who fails to 'acknowledge the enjoyment derived from the position of superiority such an act confers', and 'the gesture of saints who, for example, drank the water in which they had washed the feet of lepers' (2006: 29). In drinking the water that has been polluted by his own act of kindness, the saint is in some way acknowledging and accepting the reality of what he has done. The full implications of the leper's dangerousness have been accepted and, literally, taken in (contained) and allowed to endanger the saint. The contrast with the good Samaritan, who could engage the naked stranger but who rather hands over his coat and moves on, is great. Taubman cites Zizek to explore this:

> 'The ultimate problem in intersubjectivity is precisely the extent to which we are ready to accept the other – . . . in the real of his or her existence' (Zizek, 1998: 167). The Real of the leper, the horror bursting through the skin, is

exactly what must be accepted. To preach acceptance without accepting the real of the Other is to reduce the Other to some symbolic fiction.

(Taubman, 2006: 29–30)

In a typically jolting Lacanian move, the other is within us as well as 'out there': the unknowable 'not me' and my unknowable unconscious. Can I accept the other? And can I accept myself? Caring for generalised notions of 'needy children' is not the same as confronting the noisy, incessant and infuriatingly counterproductive demands of Rhatul and his peers in the grip of anxiety: the 'needy children' of our imaginations (and policy) are symbolic fictions.

While there may not be any leprous feet to be washed, Taubman's suggestion is that the unconscious dangerousness of the learner and of the teacher needs to be accepted and taken in within the classroom. Such unconscious dangerousness would include feelings of hate and the desire to squash heads, to make real the aggression implicit in the wish, metaphorically expressed, to *hammer* or *drum* facts into resistant learners, to *eat up* delightful children, to *kill* the learners who resist, or to *tear our hair out*. If we cannot accept the horror bursting through our own skins, how are we going to think about the horror we see bursting through the skins of others? When we are pleased with our own goodness, niceness, caring, we act like the good Samaritan giving his cloak. In doing this, we fail to acknowledge our pleasure in the acts of kindness and, in so doing, we fail to recognise our own jouissance and take possession of the other ('my children', 'my class'); we are all one. For as long as we continue to believe exclusively in our fantasies of teaching as a profession ruled by love and self-sacrifice, and the 'goodness' of our hidden controls, the delight of our own aggressive impulses and our hate will remain unacknowledged.

Being 'good-enough': disillusion, weaning, guilt and reparation

What would it mean to be a 'good-enough' rather than a 'perfect' teacher? This shift from idealisation and perfection to good-enoughness is a move from the splits of the paranoid-schizoid position to the depressive position. This move suggests an acceptance of ambivalence and a toleration of the dichotomised positions that allow us to pretend the good and bad are separable.

The notion of the good-enough mother is perhaps Winnicott's most familiar legacy. This is one summary he provides to illustrate what he means:

The good-enough mother . . . starts off with an almost complete adaptation to her infant's needs, and, as time proceeds, she adapts less and less completely, gradually, according to the infant's growing ability to deal with her failure.

The infant's means of dealing with this maternal failure include the following:

1. The infant's experience, often repeated, that there is a time-limit to frustration. At first, naturally, this time-limit must be short.
2. Growing a sense of process.
3. The beginnings of mental activity.
4. Enjoyment of auto-erotic satisfactions.
5. Remembering, reliving, fantasying, dreaming; the integrating of past, present and future.

(Winnicott, 1971: 14)

In chapter 4, I dealt in more detail with Winnicott's understanding of how the child begins to think by controlling its bodily functions and understanding that it can control and generate some of its own pleasures (auto-erotic satisfactions).[5] Winnicott's Kleinian roots are evident in the way he talks about the frustrations generated by the mother's inevitable failures to know precisely what the baby needs the instant he experiences the need and the fact that these frustrations are what stimulate thinking. In this way, the mother provides the disillusion that forces weaning. The literal weaning of the baby off the breast and onto solid food has a metaphorical equivalence in weaning the baby off its absolute dependence on his mother and onto thinking and learning to 'be' in the world. It also resonates with the need to perpetually wean the self off the comforts of the paranoid-schizoid position and onto the work of the depressive position. How then might we translate this good-enough mother into a good-enough teacher, and how might the infant's *means of dealing with maternal failure* map across onto students' behaviours in the classroom?

Complete adaptation of one to another is always a fantasy: it is for the mother, and it is for the teacher (we can never know the other's mind). Even in the presence of adult students who we might want to believe are better able to express themselves, the unconscious remains unknown and symbolisation remains slippery; communication is forever uncertain. However, we might recognise in Winnicott's developmental story an image of the institution of education.

Schooling begins in the nursery class with an apparently generous willingness to adapt to the needs of the very young child. Over time, school involves itself less and less with the needs of the 'child', expecting the learner to be more and more self-sufficient. The extreme end of this developmental journey is marked by the university which traditionally makes few concessions to the needs of the learner. Unfortunately, this parallel educational/developmental story forgets two important facts. First, the education system is not the mother, it is a collective abstraction rather than a single mindful body; and second, it privileges straightforward, linear, rational time, and the unconscious knows no such thing. Our unconscious developments are timeless; being born into a new idea can happen to anyone open to learning whatever their chronological age – and at that moment wherever they are in (or outside) the education system, they are, metaphorically speaking, babies in need of good-enough mothering, timely disillusion and weaning.

So what of Winnicott's list of the infant's responses to maternal failures? And, what possible help can these be to teachers?

(1) *The learner's experience, often repeated, that there is a time-limit to frustration. At first . . . this time-limit must be short.* Winnicott's first suggestion is that the baby/learner needs to learn that frustration can be overcome. For this to happen, early experiences of frustration need to be managed so that there are multiple experiences of the baby/learner surviving them. To begin with at least, support needs to be on hand because frustration in the face of a new idea feels extremely threatening and cannot be easily tolerated; it will initially generate fears of annihilation, disintegration, death and destruction. However, not to allow some challenge and frustration robs the learner of opportunities to learn from them and from their survival.

(2) *Growing a sense of process.* Learners can survive the teacher's lapses if they have some sense of how they learn but they will need help to develop this. Coming to recognise the places where their capacity to think, to know, to tolerate breakdown, recognising the experiences that destroy the ability to tolerate ambivalence and create frustration, is difficult. These are the moments when good and bad are created and thinking stops. Learning to see this happen is frustrating and sends us repeatedly back to the beginning and more frustration. It is the experience of always being the one who, when playing 'snakes and ladders', lands on the snake on square 99 and is transported back to square 1.

(3) *The beginnings of mental activity.* As we saw in chapter 7, this requires that frustrations be recognised and tolerated, symbolised and contained, and that the thoughts generated also be tolerated so that thinking can emerge to process them and develop new thoughts which, in their turn, require more and new tolerances. The more a learner can experience this and know they have experienced it, the more their tolerance for their teachers' failures can develop. But this awareness can never be taken for granted.

(4) *Enjoyment of auto-erotic satisfactions.* Unbearable tensions and frustrations need to be evacuated; they lead to splitting and non-thought. However, physical experiences of tension and frustration can be alleviated by 'auto-erotic' means: thumb-sucking, pencil chewing, doodling, hair twiddling, pacing the classroom. If tensions can be soothed and managed, if they can be modified rather than evaded, then reverie, dreaming, thinking might be more attainable and learning can proceed.

(5) *Remembering, reliving, fantasying, dreaming; the integrating of past, present and future.* Thought and thinking are brought about by the (re)making and tolerance of links. These processes begin in the unconscious and need space to emerge and grow: a hypnotic train journey, day-dreaming while gazing out of the window, colouring in.

Unfortunately any of these behaviours of learners might be unacceptable to teachers. The processes are slow (and, as Bion (1961) pointed out, we all hate the long and involved processes of learning from experience); fidgeting or looking vacant can seem like rejection of the teacher's 'good feeding' or a dismissal of their role. And indeed, vacant staring and fiddling can be ways of avoiding thinking. Or they may indicate the beginnings of thought. The teacher's dilemma, then, is how to read moments of reverie, of fiddling with hair, of apparent forgetting and regression. How is one to know? Well, we cannot know although we have to try:

> [A teacher] has to display all the patience and tolerance and reliability of a mother devoted to her infant; has to recognise the [learner's] wishes and needs; has to put aside other interests in order to be available and to be punctual and objective; and has to seem to want to give what is really only given because of the [learner's] needs.
>
> (Winnicott, 1947: 202)

It is only in doing this and, Winnicott goes on to suggest, in simultaneously being aware of the hate that having to do this thankless work engenders, that education can have any confidence that it might be about the needs of the learner rather than the needs of the teacher, or the needs of the teachers' manager, or the needs of local or central government.

For Klein, ambivalence, the depressive position, is arrived at through and with 'depressive anxiety': the infant fears that its sadistic attacks will destroy the loved object or that the loved object may turn and seek revenge, attacking the infant as it has attacked her. It is only when the object can be seen as a whole object (not *either* a good object *or* a bad object, but an object that is *both* good and bad, loved *and* hated) that depressive anxiety can emerge. From this anxiety flows guilt and a desire for reparation. The capacity to make reparation requires that the good object has been internalised sufficiently; that is, that the infant has some sense of itself as good: being worthy of love *and* being capable of love; that the learner has some sense of itself as good: being worthy of love/learning *and* being capable of love/learning.

Accepting loss: mourning and the work of reparation

Bearing Winnicott in mind, and reflecting again on the primary task of the school, education might be thought of as an endeavour that binds together learning and development. So we come to education's relentless need to move forwards. Development is clearly linked to notions of growth and parenting, reproduction, age and death. Ideas like these suggest that development will always evoke the anxieties that pertain to extreme intimacy: of love and loss, hate and death. The existence of these anxieties suggests that the forward rush of education can be understood as a defence against the very development it takes as part of its task. An exclusive focus on development and progress forecloses recognition of the cyclical nature of life, the decay and death that follow and that feed life and growth.

Education is driven by a need to be continually making progress: up levels, through the curriculum and the lessons, on towards playtime and the exams. The developmental story, whether the physical and intellectual development of children or adults, literal or more metaphorical, matters not: the move is forwards, the pace relentless. There is no tolerance for standing still, time for reflection can be read as time wasted, moving backwards is ultimately abhorrent. Yet every step taken forward leaves ground behind.

Part of the joy of walking at the margins of the sea or through snow is turning and seeing the trace of where one has walked. The fascination with our own footprints dissolving in the oncoming tide speaks of regret at the difficulty of recognising the traces of our passage through life. Yet, if we look, learning can provide us with opportunities to see where we have been: the earlier draft of an essay, a childish letter to a relative rediscovered in a box, a book we used to love, a painting we did on holiday. More often than not, though, what is gone is lost; most life is lived in an ephemeral blur. Jonathan Silin provides a poignant example of his own learning in this regard as he reflects on his time working in a nursery:

> Along with parents I celebrated familiar milestones – a child learns to button her coat, tie her shoelaces, or walk home from school on her own. I did not imagine that in learning a new way of being in the world, a child might also give up an old way, one that had worked for him in the past – the physical intimacy that occurs when an adult cares for his clothing or the social connection he experiences when accompanied by a caregiver on the walk home from school.
>
> (Silin, 2006: 233)

Just as it is filled with gains and progress, education is simultaneously saturated with loss. There are major losses incurred when we change location and stage of life, and small, mundane losses throughout the school day: the end of playtime, the loss of the warmth of the sun, the end of a task that took me over. There are the losses like 'the me who couldn't do my buttons up' and bigger ones, 'the me who had no qualification'. All of these challenge our identities and, while some might slide by with relative ease, others will require some mourning. For Klein, loss and mourning are part of the work of reparation, part of the work of love and of thinking and learning. Hinshelwood explains that reparation is 'a tolerance of the loss, and guilt and responsibility for the loss, while at the same time feeling that not all is lost' (1991: 148). Reparation comes with the hopeful possibility that, out of the danger that change might bring, something positive can come:

> For Klein, the work of the depressive position is the work of mourning... 'this early mourning is revived whenever grief is experienced later in life' [. . .] Mourning is an internal mourning for something dead inside, a dead or dying internal object; a repetition of innumerable earlier occasions.
>
> (Hinshelwood, 1991: 143)

The me that could not fasten my buttons is dead, the me that does not understand division is dying. These losses are to be mourned just as the me that can fasten my buttons and the me that does understand division are celebrated. Mourning requires time, it has its own cycles and phases. It is an unconscious process that will not be subjected to chronological time. What does it mean that we want to ignore the small losses and deaths that pepper the school day and the learning journey? What happens when we fail to celebrate (recognise, name, symbolise) and mourn what has been lost in all its glory (or ignominy)? One way to think about this is to notice that this is another loss, a loss of losses: we lose experiences that we might otherwise draw on in the work of linking and thinking.

Conclusion

There may be a desire to refuse the stories told in this book. Can we reject the research and all that flowed from it on a suspicion that the school was not a good school? Or that the teachers were bad teachers? I have two responses to such a desire. The first is a reminder that the school was an extremely successful school with a low turnover of highly committed staff, and the children achieved very highly in their end of KS2 SATs. The second, more generative (less defensive) response points to the splitting inherent in the language of 'good' and 'bad'. Schools and teachers, whatever their strengths and weaknesses, are complex places and people full of light and shade and deserving of thoughtful consideration, not quick judgement.

In the face of all the difficulties this book has pointed to we might want to throw our hands in the air and ask: 'Why bother? Let's give up and go and do something less challenging instead.' Or perhaps we might want to say 'Why bother?' and carry on regardless. Never mind if students get frustrated and hate us – as long as they pass their exams, who cares? I will have done my job. If my unconscious will fight my desire to think more carefully and know better, why should I try? If I can never completely know the other, what does it matter if I know nothing at all?

The siren call of the desire not to know is as much the lot of the teacher as it is of the learner – it keeps *the repressed* and the *conscious*, *us* and *them*, the *known* and the *unknown* apart, safe from the challenges of uncertainty and doubt and the pain of coming to know. Another option might be to make a gesture of grandiose love or intolerant impatience to fix all this misunderstanding and anxiety with pre-emptive questioning, probing and prompting. If I insist students or my colleagues face their desire not to know, then they will overcome it and it will not be a problem any more. But this is an aggressive and omnipotent demand; it insists that I know best, that I know their minds – and I cannot. All of these options split the good me from the bad them, or turn me into a bad me whom they will be better off without. None of these options accepts the ethical necessity of being a teacher and a learner who faces the difficulties.

Freud, writing about the first task of education, points out that a path must be found:

The child must learn to control his instincts. It is impossible to give him liberty to carry out all his impulses without restriction... Accordingly, education must inhibit, forbid and suppress and this is abundantly seen in all periods of history. But we have learnt from analysis that precisely this suppression of instincts involves the risk of neurotic illness... Thus education must find its way between the Scylla of non-interference and the Charybdis of frustration. ... An optimum must be discovered which will enable education to achieve the most and damage the least... We have to take into account the fact that the objects of our educational influence have very different innate constitutional dispositions, so that it is quite impossible that the same educational procedure can be equally good for all children.

(Freud, 1933: 149)

Charybdis and Scylla – the original 'rock and a hard place' – were mythical creatures: Charybdis an all-consuming whirlpool who, three times a day, spat out what she had destroyed, Scylla a six-headed monster with long grasping arms who could pluck sailors from their ships and eat them six at a time. Between them, these two monsters guarded a narrow strait and sailors had to choose to go closer to one or the other; there was no third way to cross the straits. Avoiding one danger brings us closer to another, risks have to be taken; this is the perilous route Freud shows teachers.

The paradoxical nature of the decisions that teachers have to make is one reason why Freud might have considered education (along with politics and psychoanalysis) to be an impossible profession – a profession in which 'one can be sure beforehand of achieving unsatisfactory results' (Freud, 1937: 248).[6] Another reason might be the need for the teacher to occupy multiple and often contradictory positions. For example, teachers must occupy the position of both teacher and learner; simultaneously they must be both the one who knows and the one who does not know: I know about the division of fractions but I do not know how you will respond to my lesson; I know how my understanding fits with other things I know but I do not know what connections you will form. You will need to help me understand your learning, I cannot come to know without your help, it is a part of the learning task that we must undertake together. If we can tolerate the difficulty and the time-consuming nature of the work needed to develop pedagogic relationships and communication then what psychoanalytic thinking might offer education becomes more hopeful.

It is psychoanalysis' provision of models and metaphors to think with that has the potential to be helpful; looking to it for answers can lead to frustration; it is no prophylactic (Freud, 1933). Any thought about what psychoanalytic thinking might offer education is likely to be personal and shifting. It does not offer easy answers or simple recipes for how to behave in classrooms; to suggest it does is to fall into the trap of systematicity and to defend against the need to think (Bass, 1998; Britzman, 2003). For me, at the moment, psychoanalysis offers not only an invitation to the hard work of thinking and making sense of being in the world, but also an invitation to the interesting and exciting work of play, creativity and education itself.

An invitation to play is not only a frivolous invitation to play games, it can also be an invitation to make associations to words, ideas, metaphors, stories, feelings, whatever comes to mind. In this mindful play, we might notice the ways in which new connections and ideas can be formed; this is a creative act. Approaching seemingly intractable educational problems with seriously playful intent can open new lines of enquiry, take our thinking elsewhere, enable us to notice things that we had previously overlooked. One aspect of the teacher's life that might benefit from a playful encounter is the notion of the pedagogic relationship. Fantasies about the unconditional love of the teacher develop an unhelpfully rosy picture of pedagogic relationships locking them into 'good' and cosy straightjackets. The rigidity of such fantasies limits action; they deny the very real difficulties (including envy and hate) that are an inevitable part of learning relationships. Playing with the idea of what a relationship could be might avoid such rigidity and the suffocating effects of sentimentality; it may help us keep the other (and our other selves) 'in mind' and open multiple channels through which two-way communication might emerge.

If pedagogic relationships can develop and sustain constructive 'holding environments' in the classroom, then compliance might be combated: our own and children's. This will require teachers, head teachers, school governors, local authority advisors (all the metaphorical mothers) to find ways to bracket out aspects of the pressures that come from outside; to provide some shield from the demands of accountability for those they are responsible for. The need to know and think about, but not to act on, difficult aspects of our psychic lives is part of the ethical knot for teachers.

An offer to engage playfully and creatively with knowledge, learners and my own understandings is an invitation to reclaim some aspects of teaching that the ruthless demands of the accountable classroom seemed to have stolen. Or perhaps I lost access to my playfulness and creativity when I submitted to the demands of accountability (can I have stolen it from myself?). Either way, accepting the invitation to re-engage comes at a price: the need to reject the psychically costly comforts of sentimentality or persecution, and to accept parts of life I may prefer to deny such as my own hate and aggression, and my own desire not to know.

Of course, the price is not a one-off payment. There are several pitfalls that wait to swallow us anew: from a Kleinian perspective, an idealisation of ambivalence and the depressive position is still an idealisation and therefore a refusal to think about something, or, to give this a Lacanian turn: we create an ideal from a lack-of-idealisation. As the unconscious is dynamic it will fight back, the process is a lifelong one, it requires eternal vigilance and an acceptance of imperfection and failure. All there is, is the need to engage and to think – this is what is real. But perhaps we also can learn to fail better.

Notes

1 An introduction

1 'Anna O' (Bertha Pappenheim) was a patient of Joseph Breuer and her case, written up by Freud in *Studies on Hysteria*, is generally taken to be the first case of psychoanalysis.

2 The Mental Health Act (2007) led to a policy document *Improving Access to Psychological Therapies* which required doctors and hospitals to implement programmes called '*Beating the Blues* for people with mild to moderate depression' and '*Fear Fighter* for people with panic and phobia'. For further aspects of the media debate see for example http://www.guardian.co.uk/lifeandstyle/2007/feb/23/healthandwellbeing.health (accessed 4 February 2010).

3 The spelling 'phantasy' is used to separate unconscious desires and wishes from conscious 'fantasy'.

4 ESRC supported. Award number RES-000-22-1272.

5 In England, a school's overall scores in Key Stage 2 SATs (statutory assessment tests in mathematics and English taken by children in the summer term of year 6) are publicly reported and form the basis of many outside judgements about the school. It is notable that the two subjects that count most towards the school's placement in the league tables (English/literacy and mathematics) were the only subjects taught in specially formed ability groups.

2 The primary task of the school?

1 I use the word 'parent' to stand for anyone fulfilling the parental role whether they are biological parents, family or close relatives who have taken responsibility for rearing the child, or foster or adoptive carers.

2 While out with his mother, two-year-old James Bulger was abducted from a Liverpool shopping centre in 1993. His body was later found on a nearby railway line and two ten-year-old boys were subsequently convicted of his killing. This case horrified the public and the arrest, trial and eventual release of his killers were all followed with great interest. (For further detail see: http://en.wikipedia.org/wiki/Murder_of_James_Bulger, or http://news.bbc.co.uk/1/hi/uk/991562.stm, last accessed 10 February 2010.)

3 Mirror, mirror on the wall: The Lacanian mirror in the classroom

1 The primary carer is always talked about as being the mother. This is a frequent criticism of psychoanalysis (see for example, Chodorow, 1999). 'Mother' needs to be understood

as referring to the first, primary caregiver – the person who is there most often and feeds the nursling baby whether at the breast or by bottle. Some writers use '(m)other' to indicate that the dynamic continues through life, replicated in other relationships.

2 I use the feminine pronoun rather than the clumsy she/he, her/his. Although both men and women teach, teaching remains a 'feminised' profession with more women than men entering the profession and remaining in the classroom.

3 Although Muhi was third-generation Bangladeshi-English.

4 Accountability: Winnicott in the playless classroom

1 Winnicott draws on a Kleinian understanding of the beginnings of symbolisation. There are strong parallels between the process as imagined here and Klein's suggestion that we need to experience a tolerable level of anxiety to begin to form symbols and therefore to learn (see chapter 2). This will come up again in chapter 7.

5 Tall poppies and shrinking violets: Freud, Foulkes and the nature of groups

1 S. H. Foulkes was born Siegmund Heinrich Fuchs but changed his name when he became a naturalised British citizen in 1938. He preferred to be known either by his surname, or 'SH' (Foulkes, 1990: 4).

2 These have some resonances with the conditions for the development of a 'true' self-structure (chapter 4): 'sense of inner safety, the management of external events, and the ability to generate spontaneous, creative gestures'.

7 When does the lesson start? Thoughts, Thinking, learning and knowing

1 'It cannot be my body that is killing me, it must be some other malign presence, I would not do this to myself.' Although, if food is refused, this is precisely what we might do.

2 It is interesting to note that, in today's terms, Dick would be described as a child with autism.

3 The algorithms and column formatting for calculations were originally developed to satisfy the demands of accountancy and commerce. For some history see, for example, McLeish (1992).

8 But I think best with my friends: Thinking in relationships

1 Although Klein talked about the infant relating to objects and part-objects, these were internal, the phantastic creations of the individual. British Object Relations theorists (themselves a diverse group) focussed more on external objects and especially the infant's first relationship with a mother. While Object Relations develops Klein's work, it differs from it in significant ways. Frosh (1999) explores the differences. See especially chapters 4 and 5.

2 The descriptions of Benjamin's work in this section were first published in: Bibby, T. (2008). The experience of learning in classrooms: moving beyond Vygotsky. In T. Brown (Ed.), *The Psychology of Mathematics Education: A Psychoanalytic Displacement*. Rotterdam: Sense.

3 Interestingly, she behaved in the same way during an interview with a member of the research team although the exchange was treated more formally and was polite throughout.

4 Since we are constitutively alienated we are also other to ourselves. See Butler (2004, especially chapter 6) for a critique of Benjamin's work.

9 Being 'good-enough' and taking the risk to 'fail better'

1 This comes from *Worstward Ho*. It is also interesting to note that Beckett undertook analysis with Bion.

2 This is also true if the assumption is one of resilience rather than vulnerability: resilience assumed and taken for granted is no better than vulnerability assumed.

3 Later in 2009 David Nutt, the government's scientific advisor, was sacked over comments about drugs policy. His sacking led to resignations from other members of the advisory panel dismayed at the government's unwillingness to listen to advice (for more detail see, for example, Toynbee, 2009).

4 Evans defines jouissance as a term that 'nicely expresses the paradoxical satisfaction that the subject derives from his symptom, or, to put it another way, the suffering that he derives from his own satisfaction (Freud's primary gain from illness)' (1996: 92). Elsewhere Elliott (2002) and Frosh (1999) draw attention to the way jouissance dissolves our notions of self and other. It takes us back to a fantasy of oneness – the unity that we want to have existed before we became aware of a 'not me' separate from 'me', a phantastic place of omnipotence, satisfied demands and complete safety. In this respect jouissance has some connection to the notion of complementarity. An important difference is that, while complementarity in relational psychoanalysis is a term with pejorative overtones, jouissance carries no judgement.

5 Chapter 7 considered these processes from Kleinian and Bionian perspectives.

6 The full quotation is: 'It almost looks as if analysis were the third of those "impossible" professions in which one can be sure beforehand of achieving unsatisfying results. The other two, which have been known much longer, are education and government.'

References

Acker, S. (1999). *The realities of teachers' work: never a dull moment*. London and New York: Cassell.

Alexander, R., with, Flutter, J., Northen, S., and Richards, C. (Eds). (2009). *Children, their world, their education: final report and recommendations of the Cambridge Primary Review*. Abingdon: Routledge.

Alexander, R., Rose, J., and Woodhead, C. (1992). *Curriculum organisation and classroom practice: a discussion paper*. London: Department of Education and Science (DES).

Alford, C. F. (1998). Melanie Klein and the nature of good and evil. In P. Marcus and A. Rosenberg (Eds), *Psychoanalytic versions of the human condition: philosophies of life and their impact on practice* (pp. 117–39). New York and London: New York University Press.

Appignanesi, L., and Forrester, J. (2005). *Freud's women*. San Francisco: Phoenix.

Atkinson, D. (2004). Theorising how student teachers form their identities in initial teacher education. *British Educational Research Journal, 30*(3), 379–94.

Ball, S. J. (1993). Education, Majorism and 'the curriculum of the dead'. *Curriculum Studies, 1*(2), 195–214.

—— (2003). The teacher's soul and the terrors of performativity. *Journal of Education Policy, 18*(2), 215–28.

—— (2008). *The education debate*. Bristol: Polity Press.

Bass, A. (1998). Sigmund Freud: the questions of a Weltanschauung and of defense. In P. Marcus and A. Rosenberg (Eds), *Psychoanalytic versions of the human condition: philosophies of life and their impact on practice* (pp. 412–46). New York and London: New York University Press.

Benjamin, J. (1988). *The bonds of love: psychoanalysis, feminism, and the problem of domination* (Vol. 1990). Reading: Virago.

—— (1998). *Shadow of the other: intersubjectivity and gender in psychoanalysis*. New York, London: Routledge.

—— (2004). Beyond doer and done to: an intersubjective view of thirdness. *Psychoanalytic Quarterly, LXXIII*, 5–46.

Bibby, T. (2002). Shame: an emotional response to doing mathematics as an adult and a teacher. *British Educational Research Journal, 28*(5), 705–22.

—— (2008). The experience of learning in classrooms: moving beyond Vygotsky. In T. Brown (Ed.), *The psychology of mathematics education: A psychoanalytic displacement*. Rotterdam: Sense.

—— (2009a). How do children understand themselves as learners? Towards a learner-centred understanding of pedagogy. *Pedagogy, Culture and Society, 17*(1), 41–56.

—— (2009b). How do pedagogic practices impact on learner identities in mathematics? A psychoanalytically framed response. In L. Black, H. Mendick, and Y. Solomon (Eds), *Mathematical relationships in education: identities and participation.* (pp. 123–35). London: Routledge.

Bion, W. R. (1961). *Experiences in groups and other papers* (2004 ed.). Hove, East Sussex: Brunner-Routledge.

—— (1967). *Second thoughts* (2006 ed.). London: Karnac.

Boldt, G. M., and Salvio, P. M. (Eds). (2006). *Love's return: psychoanalytic essays on childhood, teaching, and learning.* London: Routledge.

Bollas, C. (1999). *The mystery of things* (2001 ed.). London: Routledge.

Bracher, M. (2002). Identity and desire in the classroom. In J. Jagodzinski (Ed.), *Pedagogical desire: authority, seduction, transference and the question of ethics* (pp. 93–121). Westport CT, London: Bergin and Garvey.

Britzman, D. P. (1998). Some observations on the work of learning: a discussion paper for the Centre for Learning and Teaching, York University. *Journal of Curriculum Theorizing, 14*(2), 53–59.

—— (2003). *After-Education: Anna Freud, Melanie Klein, and psychoanalytic histories of learning.* Albany: SUNY.

—— (2009). *The very thought of education: psychoanalysis and the impossible professions.* Albany: SUNY.

Britzman, D. P., and Pitt, A. J. (1996). Pedagogy and transference: casting the past of learning into the presence of teaching. *Theory Into Practice, 35*(2), 117–23.

Burman, E. (1994). *Deconstructing developmental psychology.* London: Routledge.

—— (1997). Developmental psychology and its discontents. In D. Fox and I. Prilleltensky (Eds), *Critical psychology: an introduction* (pp. 134–49). London: Sage.

Bush, G. (2001). Bush says it is time for action. Retrieved 24 July 2009, from http://archives.cnn.com/2001/US/11/06/ret.bush.coalition/index.html

Butler, J. (1997). *The psychic life of power.* Stanford: Stanford University Press.

—— (2004). *Undoing gender.* London: Routledge.

Butler, R. (1988) Enhancing and undermining intrinsic motivation: the effect of task-involving and ego-involving evaluation of interest and performance. *British Journal of Educational Psychology 58*, 1–14

Chodorow, N. (1999). *The reproduction of mothering.* Berkeley: University of California Press.

Coaker, V. (2009). Cambridge primary review: why the government rejects it. Retrieved 9 December 2009, from http://www.guardian.co.uk/education/mortarboard/2009/oct/16/cambridge-primary-review-vernon-coaker/

Collins dictionary of the English language (2nd ed.). (1986). London: Collins.

de Sautoy, M. (2009). *The Secret You* [BBC TV]. In D. Walker (Producer), Horizon: BBC.

DfES. (2004). Every Child Matters: change for children in schools [Electronic Version], Retrieved December 2009, from http://www.everychildmatters.gov.uk/_files/07CD1E89BFFA749324DC47F707DD5B7F.pdf

Doane, J., and Hodges, D. (1993). *From Klein to Kristeva: psychoanalytic feminism and the search for the good enough mother (Critical perspectives on women and gender).* Michigan: University of Michigan Press.

Donaldson, M. (1978). *Children's minds* (1990 ed.). London: Fontana.

Ecclestone, K., and Hayes, D. (2009). *The dangerous rise of therapeutic education*. London: Routledge.

Elliott, A. (2002). *Psychoanalytic theory: an introduction*. London: Palgrave.

Elliott, A., and Frosh, S. (Eds). (1995). *Psychoanalysis in contexts: paths between theory and modern culture*. London: Routledge.

Evans, D. (1996). *An introductory dictionary of Lacanian psychoanalysis*. London: Routledge.

Fonagy, P., and Target, M. (2003). *Psychoanalytic theories: perspectives from developmental psychopathology*. London: Whurr Publishers.

Forrester, G. (2005). All in a day's work: primary teachers 'performing' and 'caring'. *Gender and Education, 17*(3), 271–87.

Foulkes, E. (1990). S. H. Foulkes: a brief memoir. In E. Foulkes (Ed.), *Selected papers of S. H. Foulkes: psychoanalysis and group analysis* (pp. 3–20). London: Karnac Books.

Foulkes, S. H. (1946). On group analysis. Reprinted in E. Foulkes (Ed.), (1990) *Selected papers of S. H. Foulkes: psychoanalysis and group analysis* (pp. 127–36). London: Karnac Books.

—— (1966). Some basic concepts in group psychotherapy. In E. Foulkes (Ed.), *Selected papers of S. H. Foulkes: psychoanalysis and group analysis* (1990 ed., pp. 151–58). London: Karnac Books.

Freud, S. (1899). Screen memories. In J. Strachey (Ed.), *The standard edition of the complete psychological works of Sigmund Freud* (Vol. III (1893–99), pp. 301–22). London: Vintage.

—— (1921). Group psychology and the analysis of the ego. In J. Strachey (Ed.), *The standard edition of the complete psychological works of Sigmund Freud* (Vol. XVIII (1920–22), pp. 65–143). London: Vintage.

—— (1923). The ego and the id. In J. Strachey (Ed.), *The standard edition of the complete psychological works of Sigmund Freud* (Vol. XIX (1923–25), pp. 3–66). London: Vintage.

—— (1926). Inhibitions, symptoms and anxiety. In J. Strachey (Ed.), *The standard edition of the complete psychological works of Sigmund Freud* (Vol. XX (1925–26), pp. 77–175). London: Vintage.

—— (1930). Civilization and its discontents. In J. Strachey (Ed.), *The standard edition of the complete psychological works of Sigmund Freud* (2001 ed., Vol. XXI (1927–31), pp. 59–145). London: Vintage.

—— (1933). Lecture XXXIV: Explanations, applications and orientations. In J. Strachey (Ed.), *The standard edition of the complete psychological works of Sigmund Freud* (Vol. XXII (1932–36), pp. 136–57). London: Vintage

—— (1937). Analysis terminable and interminable. In J. Strachey (Ed.), *The standard edition of the complete psychological works of Sigmund Freud* (Vol. XXIII (1937–39), pp. 211–53). London: Vintage.

Frosh, S. (1999). *The politics of psychoanalysis: an introduction to Freudian and post-Freudian theory (second edition)*. London: Macmillan.

—— (2002). *Key concepts in psychoanalysis*. London: The British Library.

Frosh, S., and Baraitser, L. (2008). Psychoanalysis and psychosocial studies. *Psychoanalysis, Culture & Society, 13*(4), 346–65.

Frosh, S., Phoenix, A., and Pattman, R. (2002). *Young masculinities: understanding boys in contemporary society*. Basingstoke: Palgrave.

Furedi, F. (2004). *Therapy culture: cultivating vulnerability in an uncertain age*. London: Routledge.

Garcia, R. (Writer and Producer) (2008). *In treatment*. USA: HBO.

Gargiulo, G. J. (1998). D. W. Winnicott's psychoanalytic playground. In P. Marcus and A.

Rosenberg (Eds), *Psychoanalytic versions of the human condition: philosophies of life and their impact on practice* (pp. 140–60). New York: New York University Press.

Grosz, E. (1990). *Jacques Lacan: a feminist introduction* (1998 ed.). London: Routledge.

Hey, V. (1997). *The company she keeps: an ethnography of girls' friendships*. Buckingham: Open University.

Hinshelwood, R. D. (1991). *A dictionary of Kleinain thought* (2nd ed.). London: Free Association Books.

—— (1994). *Clinical Klein*. London: Free Association Books.

Hughes, M. (1986). *Children and number: difficulties in learning mathematics*. London: Blackwell.

James, A., and James, A. L. (2004). *Constructing childhood*. Basingstoke: Palgrave Macmillan.

Jaques, D. (1984). *Learning in groups* (1991 ed.). London: Kogan Page.

Jenks, C. (2005). Childhood and transgression. In J. Qvortrup (Ed.), *Studies in modern childhood: society, agency, culture* (pp. 115–27). Basingstoke: Palgrave Macmillan.

Klein, M. (1930). The importance of symbol formation in the development of the ego. In J. Mitchell (Ed.), *The selected Melanie Klein* (1991 ed., pp. 95–111). Harmondsworth: Penguin.

—— (1946). Notes on some schizoid mechanisms. In J. Mitchell (Ed.), *The selected Melanie Klein* (1991 ed., pp. 176–200). Harmondsworth: Penguin.

Lacan, J. (2001). The mirror stage as formative of the function of the I as revealed in the psychoanalytic experience (A. Sheridan, Trans.). In *Ecrits: a selection* (pp. 1–8). London: Routledge.

Laerke, A. (1998). By means of re-membering: notes on a fieldwork with English children. *Anthropology Today, 14*(1), 3–7.

Layard, R. (2006). *Happiness: lessons from a new science*. London: Penguin.

—— (2007). Happiness and the teaching of values [Electronic Version]. *CentrePiece, 2007*. Retrieved April 2010, from http://cep.lse.ac.uk/_new/staff/person.asp?id=970.

Lucey, H. (2001). Social class, gender and schooling. In B. Francis and C. Skelton (Eds), *Investigating gender: contemporary perspectives in education* (pp. 177–87). Buckingham: Open University Press.

Lucey, H., and Reay, D. (2002). Carrying the beacon of excellence: social class differentiation and anxiety at a time of transition. *Journal of Education Policy, 17*(3), 321–36.

Lucey, H., Melody, J., and Walkerdine, V. (2003). Uneasy hybrids: psychosocial aspects of becoming educationally successful working-class young women. *Gender and Education, 15*(3), 285–99.

Ma, L. (1999). *Knowing and teaching mathematics: teachers' understanding of fundamental mathematics in China and the United States*. Mahwah, NJ: Lawrence Erlbaum Associates.

McLeish, J. (1992). *Number: from ancient civilisations to the computer*. London: Flamingo.

Mahony, P., and Hextall, I. (2003). *Reconstructing teaching: standards, performance and accountability*. London: RoutledgeFalmer.

Marcus, P., and Rosenberg, A. (Eds). (1998). *Psychoanalytic versions of the human condition: philosophies of life and their impact on practice*. New York and London: New York University Press.

Marx, G. (1959). *Groucho and me: the autobiography of Groucho Marx*. London: Victor Gollancz.

Mauthner, M. (1997). Methodological aspects of collecting data from children: lessons from three research projects. *Children & Society, 11*, 16–28.

Mayall, B. (2002). *Towards a sociology for childhood: thinking from children's lives*. Maidenhead: Open University Press.

Menzies Lyth, I. (1960). Social systems as a defense against anxiety. Reprinted in P. du Gay, J. Evans, and P. Redman (Eds), *Identity: a reader* (2000) (pp. 163–82). London: Sage in association with The Open University.

Mitchell, J. (1998). Introduction to Melanie Klein. In J. Phillips and L. Stonebridge (Eds), *Reading Melanie Klein* (pp. 11–31). London: Routledge.

Moore, A. (2000). *Teaching and learning: pedagogy, curriculum and culture*. London: RoutledgeFalmer.

—— (2004). *The good teacher: dominant discourses in teaching and teacher education*. London: RoutledgeFalmer.

—— (2006). Recognising desire: a psychosocial approach to understanding education policy and effect. *Oxford Review of Education, 32*(4), 487–503.

Morris, S. (2009, 13 October). Child abuser Vanessa George admits her crimes were 'disgusting and vile'. *The Guardian*. Retrieved January 2010, from http://www.guardian.co.uk/uk/2009/oct/13/child-abuser-vanessa-george

Moss, P., and Penn, H. (1996). *Transforming nursery education*. London: Paul Chapman.

Nitsun, M. (1996). *The anti-group: destructive forces in the group and their creative potential* (2003 ed.). Hove: Brunner-Routledge.

O'Hara, M. (2005, 30 November). Walking the happy talk. *The Guardian*. Retrieved January 2010, from http://www.guardian.co.uk/society/2005/nov/30/guardiansocietysupplement.politics

O'Loughlin, M. (2006). On knowing and desiring children. In G. M. Boldt and P. M. Salvio (Eds), *Love's return: psychoanalytic essays on childhood, teaching and learning* (pp. 185–202). London: Routledge.

Pajak, E. (1998). Exploring the 'shadow' side of teaching. *Journal of Curriculum Theorizing, 14*(2), 8–14.

Parsons, C. (2005). School exclusion: the will to punish. *British Journal of Educational Studies, 53*(2), 187–211.

Phillips, J., and Stonebridge, L. (1998). Introduction. In J. Phillips and L. Stonebridge (Eds), *Reading Melanie Klein* (pp. 1–10). London: Routledge.

Pines, M. (1994). The group-as-a-whole. In D. Brown and L. Zinkin (Eds), *The psyche and the social world: developments in group-analytic theory* (2000 ed., pp. 47–59). London: Jessica Kinksley.

Pitt, A., and Britzman, D. (2003). Speculations on qualities of difficult knowledge in teaching and learning: an experiment in psychoanalytic research. *Qualitative Studies in Education, 16*(6), 755–76.

Powell, L. C., and Barber, M. E. (2006). Savage inequalities indeed: irrationality and urban school reform. In G. M. Boldt and P. M. Salvio (Eds), *Love's return: psychoanalytic essays on childhood, teaching and learning* (pp. 33–60). London: Routledge.

Prout, A. (2005). *The future of childhood: towards the interdisciplinary study of children*. London: RoutledgeFalmer.

Pullman, P. (2003, 30 September). Lost the plot. *The Guardian*. Retrieved 11 October 2009, from http://www.guardian.co.uk/books/2003/sep/30/primaryeducation.schools/print

Qvortrup, J. (Ed.). (2005). *Studies in modern childhood: society, agency, culture*. Basingstoke: Palgrave Macmillan.

Reay, D. (2001a). 'Spice Girls', 'Nice Girls', 'Girlies' and 'Tomboys': gender discourses, girls' culture and femininities in the primary classroom. *Gender and Education, 13*(2), 153–66.

—— (2001b). Finding or losing yourself? Working-class relationships to education. *Journal of Educational Policy, 21*(16), 333–46.

—— (2002). Shaun's story: troubling discourses of white working-class masculinities. *Gender and Education, 14*(3), 221–34.

Rowling, J. K. (1998). *Harry Potter and the philosopher's stone*. London: Bloomsbury.

Rudduck, J., and Fielding, M. (2006). Student voice and the perils of popularity. *Educational Review, 58*(2), 219–31.

Shain, F. (2003). *The schooling and identity of Asian girls*. Stoke on Trent: Trentham.

Shaw, J. (1995). *Education, gender and anxiety*. London: Taylor and Francis.

Shepherd, J. (2009, 15 March). Self-esteem drive may backfire, warns expert. *The Observer*.

Sikes, P., and Piper, H. (2010). *Researching sex and lies in the classroom: allegations of sexual misconduct in schools*. London: Routledge.

Silin, J. G. (2006). Reading, writing and the wrath of my father. In G. M. Boldt and P. M. Salvio (Eds), *Love's return: psychoanalytic essays on childhood, teaching and learning* (pp. 227–41). London: Routledge.

Stonebridge, L. (1998). Anxiety in Klein: the missing witch's letter. In J. Phillips and L. Stonebridge (Eds), *Reading Melanie Klein* (pp. 190–202). London: Routledge.

Symington, J., and Symington, N. (1996). *The clinical thinking of Wilfred Bion* (2004 ed.). London: Routledge.

Taubman, P. M. (2006). I love them to death. In G. M. Boldt and P. M. Salvio (Eds), *Love's return: psychoanalytic essays on childhood, teaching and learning* (pp. 19–32). London: Routledge.

Tizard, B., and Hughes, M. (1984). *Young children learning*. London: Fontana.

Todd, S. (Ed.). (1997). *Learning desire: perspectives on pedagogy, culture and the unsaid*. New York, London: Routledge.

Toynbee, P. (2009, 27 November). Bad politicians are slave to public opinion. Good ones try to change it. *The Guardian*.

Walkerdine, V. (1984). Developmental psychology and the child-centred pedagogy: the insertion of Piaget into early education. In J. Henriques, W. Holloway, C. Urwin, C. Venn, and V. Walkerdine (Eds), *Changing the subject: psychology, social regulation and subjectivity* (pp. 153–202). London: Methuen.

Walkerdine, V., Lucey, H., and Melody, J. (2001). *Growing up girl: psychosocial explorations of gender and class*. London: Palgrave.

Winnicott, D. W. (1947). Hate in the countertransference. In M. M. R. Khan (Ed.), *Through paediatrics to psycho-analysis* (Vol. 1975, pp. 194–203). London: Hogarth Press and The Institute of Psycho-analysis.

—— (1964). *The child, the family and the outside world* (1991 ed.). London: Penguin.

—— (1971). *Playing and reality* (2008, Routledge Classics ed.). London: Tavistock Publications.

The Youth Justice Board. (2006). *A guide to anti-social behaviour orders (Ref 275335)*. London: The Home Office.

Index